Embattled Democracy

POLITICS AND POLICY IN THE CLINTON ERA

Embattled Democracy

POLITICS AND POLICY IN THE CLINTON ERA

THEODORE J. LOWI

CORNELL UNIVERSITY

AND

BENJAMIN GINSBERG

THE JOHNS HOPKINS UNIVERSITY

W.W. NORTON & COMPANY

NEW YORK • LONDON

Photograph Credits: Page 2, Courtesy of the White House; page 3, Courtesy of the White House;
page 27, © 1993, *The Washington Post*, reprinted by permission.

Library of Congress Cataloging-in-Publication Data
Lowi, Theodore J.
  Embattled democracy : politics and policy in the Clinton era / Theodore J. Lowi and Benjamin
Ginsberg.
      p.   cm.
  Title of previous ed. : Democrats return to power.
  1. United States—Politics and government—1993– .   2. Presidents—United States—Election—
1992.   3. Clinton, Bill, 1946– .   I. Ginsberg, Benjamin.   II. Title.
E885L68   1995
320.973′09′049—dc20   95-3403
                                                                              CIP

ISBN 0-393-96197-4 (pa)

W. W. Norton & Company, Inc., 500 Fifth Avenue, New York, N.Y. 10110
W. W. Norton & Company Ltd., 10 Coptic Street, London WC1A 1PU

1 2 3 4 5 6 7 8 9 0

Contents

PREFACE

In November 1992, Bill Clinton defeated George Bush to become America's first Democratic president in twelve years. With the Senate and House of Representatives remaining firmly in Democratic hands, America's era of divided government also seemed at an end. During the campaign, Clinton had called for change and articulated an ambitious policy agenda. Many observers expected the president and the Democratic Congress to work hand in hand to formulate and enact major new programs. Within a few months, however, bitter struggles had broken out, pitting the White House not only against Republicans in Congress, but also against important forces in the president's own party. Many of the president's policy initiatives were blocked or amended so thoroughly that they bore little resemblance to Clinton's original proposals.

To add to the president's woes, vicious battles developed over a number of his most important appointments; the leadership of the armed forces staged virtually an open revolt over the president's efforts to rescind the military's traditional ban on service by gay men and women; and the national news media presented a series of unflattering accounts of the inner workings of the White House. Everything seemed to be unraveling. And in 1994, everything *did* unravel. The Democrats suffered a stunning defeat as Republicans captured both houses of Congress as well as a number of state legislatures and gubernatorial offices.

This book begins with the 1992 election, discusses the first two years of the Clinton administration, analyzes the 1994 election, and examines the first months of Republican control of the 104th Congress. As we will see in Chapters 2 and 3, the problems encountered by Clinton and the Democrats point to profound changes that are taking place in American politics and in the nature of American government.

This volume is not only an analysis of contemporary political trends, but is also a continuation of our experiment in textbook publishing. It is designed to bridge the gap between the third and fourth editions of our introductory text, *American Government: Freedom and Power.* The third edition of our text was written before the 1994 election, while the fourth edition will not be available for classroom use until spring 1996. We hope that this brief volume, to be used in conjunction with the third edition, will provide readers with the most up-to-date examples and illustrations of the major themes of that book. At the same time, we hope that *Embattled Democracy* will introduce readers to the new analyses, problems, and questions posed by the third edition of *American Government.*

For helping us to undertake this experiment, we are grateful to our colleagues at W. W. Norton. Traci Nagle and Stephanie Larson were instrumental in preparing the volume. Our editor, Steve Dunn, played a critical role in developing the volume. As always, we also want to thank Roby Harrington for his support over the years.

1
Modern Governance: A History of Hope and Failure

Over the past thirty years, the history of the American presidency has been one of disappointment and failure. Of America's last six presidents, five were compelled to leave office sooner than they wished. President Lyndon Johnson, his administration wrecked by the Vietnam War, chose not to seek another term. President Richard Nixon was forced to resign over the Watergate scandal. Presidents Ford, Carter, and Bush lost in their efforts to win re-election. Only Ronald Reagan, among recent chief executives, was able to complete two full terms. And, even Reagan saw his presidency disrupted by the Iran-Contra scandal during his final two years in office.

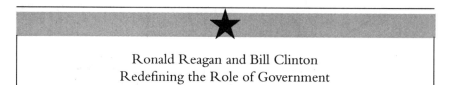

Ronald Reagan and Bill Clinton
Redefining the Role of Government

Debate over the size, scope, and power of the federal government dominated the American political agenda in the 1980s and 1990s. Ronald Reagan swept into office in 1980 in large part on the promise to reduce government. Twelve years after Reagan's election, Bill Clinton won the presidency based on his pledge to mobilize the resources of government to attack pressing domestic problems.

Ronald Reagan's career in politics extended back to his days an an actor, when he was elected president of the Screen Actors Guild in 1947. He began his political life as a Democrat but formally switched to the Republican party in 1962. He became an ardent supporter of conservative Republican Barry Goldwater's unsuccessful bid for the presidency in 1964. Two years later Reagan was elected governor of California, a position he held for eight years. In 1976, Reagan narrowly lost the Republican nomination to incumbent Gerald Ford. Four years later, he captured the nomination and the presidency on the crest of conservative enthusiasm for less government and stronger national defense spending, defeating beleaguered incumbent Jimmy Carter.

In his inaugural address, Reagan stated unequivocally that "government is not the solution to our problem; government is the problem." During his first term in office, Reagan won major revisions in fiscal policy and brought about enormous increases in military spending. During his second term, however, most of Reagan's legislative efforts were blocked by Congress, and his administration ended under the cloud of the Iran-Contra scandal. Whether viewed as a success or not, the Reagan administration redefined the American political agenda to one in which more would have to be done with less.

Although considered by many to be a supporter of big government spending, Bill Clinton sought to adapt to the post-Reagan era of limited government by redefining

Ronald Reagan

Despite this unhappy history, Americans continue to see every presidential election as an opportunity to reset the nation's course and correct the mistakes of the past. The public is generally content to listen to the promises of change and "new beginnings" during the new administration's "honeymoon" period, while even the most jaded journalists usually suspend disbelief and write paeans to the new administration's dazzling personalities, policies, and ideas. Yet five times out of six, these hopeful beginnings have ended in conflict and failure.

In November 1992, Americans again elected a new president. During Bill Clinton's first weeks in office, his popular standing was high, his relations with

---

★

the Democratic party while still drawing on the party's tradition of activism. Clinton's humble Arkansas roots belied his grand ambitions. A Rhodes scholar and graduate of Yale Law School, Clinton set his sights early on a political career. He became the nation's youngest governor when first elected in 1978. After an unexpected defeat in 1980, Clinton came back two years later to recapture the office, which he held until assuming the presidency.

Despite early political setbacks, Clinton proved to be a tenacious and durable campaigner for the 1992 presidential nomination. By the time he won the Democratic nomination, he stood even with his two rivals, George Bush and Ross Perot. From the end of the Democratic convention to election day, Clinton never trailed in the polls. Sensing that the mood of the country called for governmental leadership to address such pressing domestic problems as economic decline, revamping the nation's creaking health care system, and improving America's competitiveness, Clinton promised in his inaugural address to "resolve to make our government a place for what Franklin Roosevelt called bold, persistent experimentation."

Once in office, Clinton introduced an ambitious package of proposals, including tax and spending increases, changes in America's health care system, and reform of campaign finance and lobbying practices. His proposals were initially greeted with enthusiasm by the media, the public, and members of his own party in Congress. Within several months, however, Clinton faced intense opposition from the Republicans, large segments of the media, and even from key congressional Democrats. Analysts asked whether Clinton's difficulties resulted from the president's own errors or whether they reflected some of the more systemic problems faced by America's government today. Is government the problem as Reagan suggested? Or the solution as Clinton contends? The debate continues. . . .

Source: John Chubb and Paul Peterson, eds., *Can Government Govern?* (Washington, D.C.: The Brookings Institution, 1989).

Bill Clinton

Congress excellent. The media were describing him as the most skillful politician in America. Indeed, some members of the media compared him favorably to Roosevelt and Lincoln.

Alas, after only a very brief period in office, Clinton's popular standing had plummeted; after only six months it was the lowest of any modern president at a comparable point in his term. His major policy initiatives were in deep trouble in Congress, and the national media were characterizing him as without leadership ability, as inept and lacking a moral compass. Instead of comparing him *favorably* to Roosevelt and Lincoln, the media began comparing him *unfavorably* to George Bush—a president whom the media had previously likened to the hapless Herbert Hoover and James Buchanan.

In November 1994, Clinton's unpopularity contributed to a stunning Democratic defeat in the congressional elections, when Republicans won control of both houses of Congress for the first time since 1946. Led by the new House Speaker, Representative Newt Gingrich of Georgia, Republicans unveiled their own ambitious policy agenda aimed at scaling back the federal government. Many Democrats distanced themselves from the president and speculated openly about the likelihood that he would be dropped from the party's 1996 ticket.

What explains this history of hope and failure? Over the past several decades a new political pattern has emerged in the United States, one characterized by low rates of voter turnout, weak political parties, a central role for interest groups and the media, and the use of powerful new weapons of political warfare. These new patterns, as we shall see, are themselves part of a larger political transformation. As we approach the twenty-first century, one epoch of American political history is coming to an end and a new one is beginning. For better or worse, America is leaving the era of politics and entering the age of governance. Before we consider these broader issues, however, let us look at the Democratic party's victory in the 1992 election, the problems President Clinton encountered during his first two years in office, the Republican party's sweep of the 1994 election, and the first few months of the Republican-controlled Congress.

NATIONAL PARTY POLITICS, 1968–1992

The roots of both the Democratic win in 1992 and the Republican victory in 1994 can be traced back to the late 1960s to events that helped to reshape both major American political parties. From the 1930s through the mid-1960s, the Democratic party was the nation's dominant political force, led by a coalition of Southern white politicians and Northern urban machine bosses and labor leaders. The party drew its votes primarily from large cities, from the South, and from minorities, unionized workers, Jews, and Catholics.

Though occasionally winning presidential elections and, less often, control of Congress, the Republicans had been the nation's minority party since Franklin Roosevelt's presidential victory and the beginnings of the "New Deal" in 1933. The Republicans were led by Northeastern and Midwestern Protestants with deep roots in the business community. They drew their support primarily from middle- and upper-middle-class suburban voters from the Northeast, from rural areas, and from the small towns and cities of the Midwest.

In the 1960s, two powerful tidal waves brought about the reconstruction of both national party coalitions: the anti-Vietnam War movement and the Civil Rights movement. The anti-Vietnam War movement galvanized liberal activists in the Democratic party. These activists attacked and, during the late 1960s, destroyed much of the power of the machine bosses and labor leaders who had been so prominent in Democratic party affairs. Liberal activists organized a number of "public interest" groups to fight on behalf of such liberal goals as consumer and environmental regulation; an end to the arms race; expanded rights and opportunities for women, gays and lesbians, and the physically disabled; and gun control. These groups supported the election of liberal congressional and presidential candidates, as well as legislation designed to achieve their aims. Their efforts were quite effective; during the 1970s liberal forces in Congress were successful in enacting significant pieces of legislation in many of these areas.

For its part, the Civil Rights movement attacked and sharply curtailed the power of the Southern white politicians who had been the third leg of the Democratic party's leadership troika. In addition, the Civil Rights movement enfranchised millions of African American voters in the South, nearly all of whom could be counted upon to support the Democrats. These developments dramatically changed the character of the Democratic party.

First, the new prominence and energy of liberal activists in the Democratic party after the late 1960s greatly increased the Democratic advantage in local and congressional elections. Democrats had usually controlled Congress and a majority of state and local offices since the New Deal, and therefore already possessed an edge in elections because of the benefits of incumbency. Because incumbents have many electoral advantages, more often than not they are able to secure re-election. Particularly advantageous, of course, is the ability of incumbents to bring home "pork" in the form of federal projects and spending in their districts. In general, the more senior the incumbent, the more pork he or she can provide for constituents. Thus incumbency perpetuated Democratic power by giving voters a reason to cast their ballots for the Democratic candidate regardless of issues and ideology.

Democrats were also far more successful than Republicans even in contests to fill open congressional and local seats, for which no candidate possessed the advantage of incumbency. Until recent years, at least, these races tended to be fought on the basis of local rather than national issues. Victory, moreover, depended upon the capacity of candidates to organize armies of volunteers to hand out leaflets, call likely voters, post handbills, and engage in the day-to-day efforts needed to mobilize constituent support.

Their armies of liberal activists gave Democratic candidates a ready-made infantry force on the ground that the Republicans could seldom match. Even when incumbent Democrats died or retired, therefore, their seats were usually won by other Democrats. In this way, Democratic control of Congress was perpetuated for decades. Moreover, because the Democratic activists who were so important in congressional races were liberals who tended to favor like-minded candidates, the prominence of somewhat left-of-center forces within the Democratic congressional delegation increased markedly after the 1960s.

The same liberal activism, however, that helped propel the Democrats to victory in congressional elections often became a hindrance in the presidential electoral arena. Particularly after the 1968 Democratic presidential convention and the party's adoption of new nominating rules, liberal activists came to play a decisive role in the selection of Democratic presidential candidates. Although liberal Democrats were not always able to nominate the candidate of their choice, they were in a position to block the nomination of candidates they opposed.

The result was that the Democratic nominating process often produced candidates who were considered too liberal by much of the general electorate. This perception contributed to defeat after defeat for Democratic presidential candidates. In 1972, for example, Democratic candidate George McGovern suffered an electoral drubbing at the hands of Republican Richard Nixon after proposing to decrease the tax burden of lower-income voters at the expense of middle- and upper-income voters. Similarly, in 1984, Walter Mondale was routed by Ronald Reagan after pledging to increase taxes and social spending if elected.

The Democratic party's difficulties in presidential elections were compounded by the aftermath of the Civil Rights movement. The national Democratic party had helped to bring about the enfranchisement of millions of black voters in the South. To secure the loyalty of these voters, as well as to cement the loyalty of black voters in the North, the national Democratic leadership supported a variety of civil rights and social programs designed to serve the needs of African Americans.

Unfortunately, however, the association of the national Democratic party with civil rights and the aspirations of blacks alienated millions of white Democrats, including Southerners and blue-collar Northerners, who felt that black gains came at their expense. White voters defected en masse to support George Wallace's third-party presidential candidacy in 1968. Subsequently, many began voting for Republican presidential candidates.

Efforts by Democratic presidential candidates to rebuild their party's support among Southern whites and blue-collar Northerners were hampered by the harsh racial arithmetic of American politics. In the wake of the Voting Rights Act, the Democratic party depended upon African Americans for more than 20 percent of its votes in national presidential elections. Yet at the same time, and for a more or less equal percentage of votes, the Democrats relied upon whites who, for one or another reason, were unfriendly to blacks. Efforts by Democratic candidates to bolster their support among blacks by focusing on civil rights and social programs wound up losing them as much support among whites as they gained among blacks. Conversely, those Democratic candidates who avoided overtly courting black support in order to maintain white backing were hurt by declines in black voter turnout. For example, in 1984, Walter Mondale assiduously courted black support and was abandoned by Southern white Democrats. In 1988, Michael Dukakis carefully avoided too close an association with blacks, and was punished by a steep decline in black voter turnout.

Thus, liberal activism and civil rights combined to weaken the Democratic party in national presidential elections. From 1968 on, the Republicans moved swiftly to take advantage of this weakness. Their presidential candidates developed a number of issues and symbols designed to show that the Democrats were too liberal and too eager to appease blacks at the expense of whites. For instance, be-

ginning in 1968, Republicans emphasized a "Southern strategy," consisting of opposition to school busing to achieve racial integration and resistance to affirmative action programs.

At the same time, Republicans took on a number of issues and positions designed
to distinguish their own candidates from what they declared to be the excessive
liberalism of the Democrats. Republican platforms included support for school
prayer and opposition to abortion, advocacy of sharp cuts in taxes on corporations
and on middle- and upper-income voters, a watering-down of consumer and environmental federal regulatory programs, efforts to reduce crime and increase
public safety, and increased spending on national defense. Accordingly, during the
Reagan and Bush presidencies, taxes were cut, defense spending increased, regulatory efforts reduced, support for civil rights programs curtailed, and at least token
efforts made to restrict abortion and reintroduce prayer in the public schools.

These Republican appeals and programs proved quite successful in presidential
elections. Southern and some Northern blue-collar voters were drawn to the
Republicans' positions on issues of race. Socially conservative and religious voters
were energized and mobilized in large numbers by the Republicans' strong opposition to abortion and support for school prayer. Large numbers of middle- and
upper-middle-class voters were drawn to Republicanism by tax cuts. The business
community responded positively to Republican efforts to reduce the government's regulatory efforts and to the prospect of continuing high levels of defense
spending. These issues and programs carried the Republicans to triumph in five
of six presidential contests between 1968 and 1992. The South and West, in particular, became Republican strongholds in presidential elections and led some analysts to assert that the Republicans had a virtual "lock" on the Electoral College.

Nevertheless, the issues that allowed the Republicans to achieve such an impressive record of success at the presidential level during this period still did not
translate into GOP victories in the congressional, state, or local races. Presidential
races are mainly media campaigns in which opposing forces compete for the attention and favor of the electorate through television spot ads, media events, and
favorable press coverage. This form of politics emphasizes the use of issues and
symbols. Congressional and local races, by contrast, were typically fought "on the
ground" by armies of volunteers. The national media could devote little attention
to any individual local race, while local media tended to focus on local issues and
personalities. As a result, national issues, for the most part, had little effect upon
the outcomes of local races.

Frequently, Democratic members of Congress, making vigorous use of the
federal pork barrel, won handily in the same districts that were carried by the
Republican presidential candidate. Presidential and congressional elections
seemed to exist in different political universes. Voters who supported a Richard
Nixon or a Ronald Reagan at the presidential level seemed still to love their
Democratic congressional representatives.

Senatorial elections have some of the characteristics of national races and
some of the characteristics of local races. Both media and activists can be important. Therefore, though Republicans had greater success in capturing the White
House than the Senate, they had a better record in Senate races than in contests
for the House.

Thus, for thirty years, the pattern of American politics was Republican control of the White House and Democratic control of Congress, especially of the House of Representatives. Indeed, this pattern seemed to have become such a permanent feature of the American political landscape that each party began to try both to fortify its own institutional stronghold and to undermine its opponent's. Democrats sought to strengthen Congress while weakening the presidency. Republicans tried to expand presidential powers while limiting those of Congress.

For this reason, Democratic congresses enacted such legislation as the War Powers Act, the Budget and Impoundment Control Act, and the Arms Export Control Act, all of which sought to place limits upon the use of presidential power at home and abroad. In a similar vein, the Ethics in Government Act gave Democratic congresses a mechanism for initiating formal investigations and even the prosecution of executive branch officials—usually Republican appointees. The Iran-Contra investigations, for example, led to indictments of a number of high-ranking Republicans.

For their part, Republicans sought to weaken Congress with sharp cuts in the domestic spending programs upon which congressional Democrats rely to build constituency support. Republicans also built a record of successful presidential *faits accomplis* in foreign affairs, such as the Reagan administration's invasion of Grenada and bombing of Libya. The favorable popular reaction to these presidential initiatives undermined the War Powers Act and untied the hands of the White House in foreign and military affairs.

Although engaged in these sorts of institutional struggles, each party also sought to devise strategies to capture its opponent's political base. Moderate and conservative Democrats argued that the party could win presidential elections if it nominated an ideologically centrist candidate who ran on issues that would appeal to the middle-class voters who had rejected more liberal Democratic nominees. Moderate Democrats organized the Democratic Leadership Council (DLC), which sought to develop new issues and advance the political fortunes of moderate candidates. Many Democrats also advocated a version of the GOP's "Southern strategy," arguing that a moderate Southerner would be the party's ideal presidential candidate. Such an individual not only might attract middle-class voters in the North, but also might lead Southern whites, who had defected to the Republicans in presidential elections, to return to their Democratic roots.

While Democrats pondered ways in which they might capture the presidency, some Republicans considered strategies that might allow them to storm the seemingly impregnable Democratic fortress on Capitol Hill. In the 1970s and 1980s, the Republican National Committee (RNC) embarked upon an effort to recruit politically attractive candidates for congressional and local races. The RNC also sought to create a national fundraising apparatus to replace, or at least augment, the historically decentralized fundraising that characterized both American political parties. The RNC was able to create a nationwide direct-mail fundraising machine that allowed it to raise millions of dollars through small contributions. These funds could then be allocated to those local races where they might do the most good.

At the same time, Republicans began to reach out to anti-abortion forces and religious conservatives. These groups represented important voting blocs. Even more important, however, was the possibility that the religious fervor of these groups could be converted into political activism. If so, these forces could become a source of Republican volunteers and activists in the same way that the fervent anti-Vietnam forces fueled Democratic activism for years. In other words, religious conservatives could give the Republicans the infantry needed to compete effectively in local and congressional races.

Finally, Republican strategists looked for ways to "nationalize" congressional and local races. For thirty years, issues such as taxes, defense, and abortion had brought the GOP victory in presidential contests. Yet, these issues did not appear to have much impact at the sub-presidential level. Indeed, local Democratic candidates usually tried to avoid identification with national issues and ideologies, calculating that they could only be hurt by them. The question for Republicans, then, was how to tie popular local Democrats to the national party's often unpopular issues and ideological stances.

The Democratic Southern/moderate strategy produced two presidential victories: the election of Jimmy Carter in 1976, and the election of Bill Clinton in 1992. Carter seemed to be the ideal Democratic candidate. He was a white Southerner with a good civil rights record. His political views seemed to be centrist. Carter's victory over incumbent Republican Gerald Ford led some Democrats to hope that their party's presidential problems were over.

Unfortunately, however, the moderate bent that allowed Carter to win the presidential election proved a handicap in office. Carter's middle-of-the-road programs and policies alienated liberal Democrats in Congress, who quickly attacked his presidency. Liberals were so offended by what they saw as Carter's conservative leanings that they supported a fierce challenge to his renomination in 1980 and gave him only lukewarm support against Reagan in the general election. Liberal Democrats, it would seem, supported the idea of a centrist campaign but did not go so far as to support a centrist administration. The party's liberal wing had what appeared to be incompatible goals: they wanted a centrist campaign that would win the election, followed by a liberal administration to govern the nation. In 1992, a solution to this dilemma seemed to be at hand.

THE 1992 ELECTION

By the end of George Bush's term in office the Reagan coalition had begun to unravel. The two key elements in the electoral appeal of Reaganism had been prosperity at home and strength abroad. But by 1992, these two key elements were gone. The nation was mired in one of the longest economic downturns in recent decades, and the Soviet Union had collapsed, bringing an end to the cold war and diminishing the threat of a nuclear holocaust.

Between 1989 and 1992, virtually every indicator of economic performance told the same story: rising unemployment, declining retail sales and corporate profitability, continuing penetration of American markets by foreign firms and the loss of American jobs to foreigners, a sharp drop in real estate prices followed by a wave of bank collapses, and large numbers of business failures. The poor performance of the American economy during his term in office eroded Bush's popularity and divided the Republican coalition. Business groups that had supported the Republicans since the 1970s began to desert the GOP. During the 1970s, most businesses had perceived government as a threat, fearing that consumer and environmental legislation, which were supported by the Democrats, would be enormously costly and burdensome. Reagan's call for "deregulation" was a major source of the enthusiastic and virtually unanimous support he received from the business community.

By 1992, however, economic hardship compelled small and medium-sized businesses to seek governmental assistance rather than worry about the threat of excessive governmental regulation. In particular, firms facing severe foreign competition in domestic and world markets sought government aid in the form of protection of their domestic markets coupled with vigorous governmental efforts to promote their exports. As a result, the political unity of American business brought about by Reagan was shattered and a major prop of the Republican coalition undermined.

Economic hardship also drove away blue-collar support for the Republican coalition. Traditionally, blue-collar voters had been tied to the Democratic party on the basis of that party's economic stands. During the 1980s, however, Reagan and Bush won the support of many of these voters in both the North and the South by persuading them to put their economic interests aside and to focus instead on their moral and patriotic concerns.

A major function of the Republican "social agenda" of opposition to abortion, support for prayer in the public schools, and unabashed patriotism was to woo blue-collar voters from the Democratic camp by convincing them to regard themselves as right-to-lifers and patriots rather than as workers. Similarly, Republican opposition to affirmative action and school busing was designed to appeal to blue-collar Northerners as well as to traditionally Democratic Southerners offended by their party's liberal positions on matters of race.

By 1992, however, the political value of the social agenda had diminished. Faced with massive layoffs in many key industries, blue-collar voters could no longer afford the luxury of focusing on moral or racial issues rather than on their economic interests. In a number of states, as a result, the racial issues of the 1980s lost their political potency.[1] Indeed, even patriotism gave way to economic concerns as the recession lengthened. This was why George Bush's incredible 91 percent approval rating following the Persian Gulf War fell by as much as 50 points in less than one year. During the 1980s and early 1990s, millions of working-class voters who became unemployed or were forced to find lower-paying jobs deserted the Republican camp.

Middle-class executives and professionals, who are usually fairly well insulated from the economic downturns that often devastate blue-collar workers, also felt the impact of the economic crises of the late 1980s and early 1990s. The cumulative effect of the mergers and acquisitions of the 1980s, the failure of hundreds of banks, corporate restructuring and "downsizing," the massive shift of manufactur-

[1]For a discussion of events in one state, see David Broder, "In North Carolina, Racially Coded Wedge Issues No Longer Dominate," *Washington Post*, 13 October 1992, p. A12.

ing operations out of the country, the decline of the securities industry, the col-

lapse of the housing market, and the end of the defense boom meant at least the
possibility of unemployment or income reduction for hundreds of thousands of
white-collar, management, and professional employees. Even those whose jobs
were secure saw their economic positions eroded by the sharply declining values
of their homes.

Economic hard times gave middle-class voters another reason for alarm. One
of the inevitable consequences of economic distress and unemployment is an increase in crime rates. During the late 1980s and early 1990s, crime rates throughout the United States soared. In 1980, middle-class taxpayers had responded
favorably to Ronald Reagan's call for a cap on social spending coupled with a
tough approach to crime. For twelve years, limits on domestic social spending
were a cornerstone of the Republican program. In 1992, however, rising crime
rates despite Republican "get tough" rhetoric allowed the Democrats to persuade
many middle-class voters that the expansion of domestic social spending was a
price that had to be paid for the preservation of social peace and public safety.

Thus, the decline of prosperity at home caused cracks in the Reagan coalition. Under the pressure of economic distress, groups that had been enthusiastic
supporters of Reaganism in the early 1980s broke away from the GOP in 1992.

While the constituency for the Republican social agenda shrank, the moral
fervor of the groups most fiercely committed to those issues grew nonetheless.
When right-to-life forces launched protests and sought to block the doors of
abortion clinics across the nation, President Bush saw no choice but to endorse
strongly the activities of these loyal Republicans. However, Bush's support for
these groups hurt his standing among rank-and-file Republicans. The Republican
party's traditional suburban, upper-middle-class constituency had never been enthusiastic about the social agenda or about the sorts of people it had brought into
the party. As the 1992 campaign approached, Bush suffered a considerable loss of
support in this stratum, a loss that was only exacerbated by the prominent role as-
signed to social conservatives at the 1992 Republican convention.

To compound the Republican party's woes, the unity of its coalition was also
undermined by the collapse of the Soviet Union and the end of the cold war
threat. Particularly when coupled with the poor performance of the American
economy, the collapse of the Soviet Union made it impossible for the Republicans to continue to insist on the primacy of international and security issues.
Once the threat of war had receded, Americans were freer than they had been in
years to focus on problems at home. As a result, working-class voters who had
been persuaded to support the GOP despite economic interests that had historically linked them to the Democrats now began to reassess their positions. Many
patriots became workers once again.

Thus, the collapse of the Soviet Union undermined the second key element of
the Republican coalition's political success. For twelve years, the Republicans had
emphasized prosperity at home and strength abroad. Now, in 1992, the nation was
not prosperous, and its unprecedented military strength seemed irrelevant.

As the loyalty of the forces brought into the Republican camp by Reaganite
appeals began to wane, President Bush found himself increasingly dependent on a
core Republican constituency of hard-line social and political conservatives. Bush

calculated that he had to maintain his support on the political right in order to have any chance of re-election. For this reason, he gave conservatives, including his nemesis from the presidential primaries, Patrick Buchanan, a significant role in the 1992 Republican National Convention, gave their views a prominent place in the Republican platform, and emphasized "family values" in his presidential campaign. All this helped to strengthen Bush's support on the right. Unfortunately for Bush, his efforts to placate the Right led to unease among moderate Republicans whose support for the president was already wavering under the pressure of economic and world events.

The Presidential Campaign

These cracks in the Republican coalition provided the Democrats with their best opportunity in two decades to capture the White House. First, however, they had to put their own party's house in order. Since the early 1970s, Democratic candidates had been handicapped by a liberal ideology. During this period, moderate Democrats had argued that the party needed to present a more centrist image if it hoped to be competitive in national elections. The major organizational vehicle for the centrists was the Democratic Leadership Council (DLC), an organization based in Washington, D.C., and funded by businesses with ties to the Democratic party. Throughout the Reagan and Bush years, the DLC organized networks of state and local party officials and sought to develop political themes that could both bring about a measure of party unity *and* appeal to the national electorate.[2]

In 1992, the DLC and its moderate allies were able to dominate the Democratic party's presidential nominating processes as well as its national convention. The party chose as its presidential and vice presidential candidates Governor Bill Clinton of Arkansas and Senator Al Gore of Tennessee, both founding members of the DLC. The platform adopted at the party's national convention was widely perceived to be the most conservative in decades, stressing individual responsibility and private enterprise, while implicitly criticizing welfare recipients. Though the platform mentioned the importance of protecting the rights of women, gays, and minorities, gone were the calls for expanded rights for criminal and welfare recipients that had provided Republicans with such convenient political targets in previous years.

Democrats sought to deal with their party's racial divisions by keeping African American politicians and racial issues at arm's length and relying upon economic appeals to woo both working-class white and black voters. Democratic strategists calculated that black voters and politicians would have no choice but to support the Democratic ticket. Given the nation's economic woes, which afflicted blacks even more than whites, Democratic leaders reasoned that they did not need to appeal explicitly for black support. This freed the party to seek the votes of conservative whites. One step in this direction was, of course, the creation of a ticket headed by two Southerners. Democrats hoped that the Clinton-Gore ticket would appeal directly to the Southern white voters who once had been Demo-

---

[2]For a discussion, see Thomas Edsall, "The Democrats Pick a New Centerpiece," *Washington Post National Weekly Edition,* 24 August 1992, p. 14.

cratic stalwarts, but who had made the Deep South a Republican bastion during

the Reagan years.

Clinton went out of his way to assure conservative whites in both the North and South that, unlike previous Democratic candidates, he would not cater to blacks. He thus became the first Democratic presidential candidate in two decades who was neither burdened by an excessively liberal image nor plagued by the party's racial division. With Democratic strategists believing they had stabilized the party's traditional Southern, African American, and blue-collar base, Clinton and his allies moved to expand into Republican electoral territory. For this purpose, the Democrats fashioned an economic message designed to appeal to business and middle-class interests without alienating the party's working-class constituency.

Against the backdrop of continuing economic recession and Republican disarray, the Democrats' economic program and new posture of moderation on racial issues and ideology helped the Clinton-Gore ticket take a commanding lead in the polls in August 1992, after the Democratic National Convention. The Republican ticket's difficulties became evident during the nationally televised presidential and vice presidential debates in October. While the Democratic candidates focused on the nation's economic distress, constantly reminding voters of the need for programs and policies designed to improve the nation's economy, George Bush and Dan Quayle had considerable difficulty articulating an affirmative message and were left to talk about character. Not surprisingly, the debates attracted few new voters to the Republican camp.

Complicating the debates, and the 1992 campaign more generally, was the peculiar candidacy of billionaire businessman H. Ross Perot. Initially, Perot's blunt, no-nonsense, can-do style generated considerable enthusiasm among voters apparently tired of mainstream politicians. Perot made extremely effective use of television talk shows and call-in programs such as "Larry King Live" to present himself as an ordinary American tired of the inability of politicians to resolve the nation's many problems. By mid-June, both major-party candidates began to assess the potential damage of a Perot candidacy. For their part, pundits began to discuss the possibility that, for the first time since 1824, an election might be thrown into the House of Representatives if a strong Perot showing prevented either major-party candidate from obtaining the electoral college majority needed to capture the White House.

On the last day of the Democratic National Convention, however, Perot surprised his supporters by withdrawing from the race. Just over two months later, Perot muddied the political waters once again by reentering the race, supposedly at the behest of his supporters. Analysts initially greeted Perot's return with skepticism, believing that he could no longer have much impact on the election. However, Perot soon reestablished himself as a formidable figure, performing extremely well in the three presidential debates and again impressing voters as a plainspoken man of action. On November 3, Perot captured nearly 19 percent of the popular vote. This was the best showing for an independent presidential bid since Theodore Roosevelt's Bull Moose candidacy in 1912. Perot carried no states, however, and appeared to draw support away from Clinton and Bush in roughly equal percentages. Thus, despite its sound and fury, the Perot campaign ultimately had little effect upon the outcome of the election.

More than anything else, the Perot episode revealed the weakness of America's two-party system. Many voters had grown so disenchanted with established politicians and parties, and so distrustful of their promises, that they were willing to consider electing an enigmatic and mercurial outsider to the nation's highest office. To many Americans, Perot seemed to be the savior on horseback who would somehow end the stalemate, corruption, and ineptitude plaguing the nation. Citizens, of course, look to such saviors when they lose confidence in the political process and even, perhaps, in democratic politics itself. The strength of the Perot candidacy was a symptom of popular disaffection. America's political leadership must take this disaffection seriously even if its most recent symptom goes away.

After the long and arduous campaign, the election was almost anticlimactic. Still, for the first time in twelve years, the Democrats managed to oust the Republicans from the White House. The Clinton-Gore ticket achieved a comfortable victory, winning 43 percent of the popular vote and 370 electoral votes, while Bush and Quayle received 38 percent of the popular vote and only 168 electoral votes.

According to national exit-poll results reported by the *Washington Post* immediately after the election, the single issue with the largest impact upon the election's outcome was the economy.[3] Nearly half the voters surveyed cited jobs and the economy as their central concerns, and these voters supported the Democrats by a 2-to-1 margin. Among voters who felt that their own economic prospects were worsening, Clinton won by a 5-to-1 margin.

"Family values," a major Republican campaign theme, was of concern to only one voter in seven. Similarly, only one voter in twelve cited foreign policy as a major worry. The once-powerful Republican tax issue had completely lost its potency in the face of Bush's failure to adhere to his own pledge never to raise taxes. Only one voter in seven cited taxes as an important issue. Twenty percent of those surveyed said that Bush's failure to keep his promise on taxes was "very important."

At the same time, the Democrats' racial strategy—to ignore blacks and to court conservative whites—proved to be successful. Conservative white voters in the North and South responded positively to Clinton's well-publicized conflicts with Jesse Jackson and other Clinton gestures designed to distance himself from blacks. For their part, African American voters supported the Democratic ticket in overwhelming numbers, helping Clinton carry a number of Southern states.

Congressional Elections

Although some Democrats were disappointed that Clinton's victory did not translate into a gain of congressional seats for the party, the 1992 election nevertheless perpetuated the strong grip on Congress, particularly in the House of Representatives, that the Democrats had maintained through several Republican presidencies. Three developments over the previous three decades had enabled the Democrats to entrench themselves in office.

[3]Thomas B. Edsall and E. J. Dionne, Jr., "Younger, Lower-Income Voters Spurn GOP," *Washington Post,* 4 November 1992, p. 1.

First, during the 1960s and 1970s, Congress enacted a large number of new programs for local economic development, housing, hospital construction, water and air pollution control, education, and social services. These programs made available tens of billions of dollars each year that members of Congress could channel into their constituencies. By using their influence over the allocation of these funds, incumbent representatives and senators could build political support for themselves at home. In this way, incumbents greatly enhanced their prospects for re-election. Since the Democrats held a solid majority in Congress when this process began, it helped to perpetuate their control.

Second, the flow of billions of federal dollars to state and local governments and nonprofit organizations has expanded the number and influence of individuals associated with the public and nonprofit sectors throughout the country. These men and women have a strong stake in the continuation of high levels of federal funding for domestic programs and, therefore, in the election of congressional candidates with such a commitment. Although Republicans in Congress can usually be counted upon to pursue existing federal dollars for their districts, Democratic representatives are more likely to support new federal domestic initiatives as well as greater expenditures on current programs. Hence, Democratic congressional candidates throughout the nation—both newcomers and incumbents—are usually able to recruit large numbers of talented individuals from the public and nonprofit sectors to work in their campaigns. As a result, the Democrats traditionally had a reach, depth, and institutional base throughout the nation that was unmatched by the Republicans. In presidential contests, which are fought mainly in the media, campaign workers are not of decisive importance. In lower-visibility congressional, state, and local elections, however, they can be, and so the greater depth of the Democratic party is of particular importance here. Senate races lie somewhere in between, which helps to explain why the Republicans were at less of a disadvantage in Senate than House elections.

Finally, because members of Congress devote so much effort to maximizing the flow of federal benefits to their constituencies, voters have come to judge congressional candidates largely in terms of their ability to deliver these benefits. While voters expect presidential candidates to articulate national interests, they want their own representatives to protect their particular interests. As discussed above, congressional Democrats have, on the whole, been more effective in this respect than their Republican colleagues. Thus, while electing Republican presidential candidates who promise to slash domestic spending, voters have traditionally returned congressional Democrats who could be counted upon to fight for more federal dollars for their own favorite programs.

CLINTON'S FIRST TWO YEARS: TRIUMPH AND DISAPPOINTMENT

On January 20, 1993, Bill Clinton became the first Democratic president in twelve years. Clinton faced daunting problems. In a sense, his administration was haunted by two ghosts—the legacies of Ronald Reagan and James Madison.

Reagan had blocked any opportunity for new domestic programs by saddling the nation with an enormous budget deficit. Madison had left every American president with the separation of powers, an arrangement of dependence among the three branches of government that often seems to thwart all action.

Nevertheless, public expectations were high. Clinton had promised to dazzle the nation with a bevy of new programs and initiatives during his first one hundred days in office. Deficit reduction, health care reform, campaign finance reform, a tax cut for the middle class, changes in welfare policy, a new trade policy, a "reinvention" of government to make it more effective and efficient, and a host of other dramatic policy innovations had all been promised by the new administration.

Members of Congress, many serving for the first time, eagerly pledged to cooperate with the administration. James Madison's ghost seemed, for the time at least, to have fled the capital. Thousands of enthusiastic young Clintonite "policy wonks" descended on Washington, D.C., hoping to help bring about a new political era. Within a few short months, however, these dreams of rapid change had given way to a more sober understanding of the realities of American government and the limits of the politically possible.

Clinton had used a centrist campaign strategy to bring about an electoral victory in 1992. Once in office, however, he shifted to a more liberal stance to avoid losing the support of his own party, as Jimmy Carter had. As many commentators observed, Clinton "ran right but governed left." Some critics, like Representative (and now Speaker of the House) Newt Gingrich, charged that Clinton was only showing his true, "Great Society, counterculture, McGovernick" colors. Clinton's shift, however, can be better understood as a matter of political calculus than as one of personal predilection. Clinton seemed willing to do whatever worked. As he quickly realized, he could not govern without the support of the powerful liberal wing of the Democratic party in Congress.

To be sure, the extent of Clinton's shift should not be overstated. A number of the new president's policies were decidedly centrist and even won the support of the business community and broad segments of the Republican party. Clinton allied himself with congressional Republicans to secure the passage of the North American Free Trade Agreement (NAFTA), which promised to create new business opportunities for American firms. In 1994, barriers to interstate banking were relaxed with the expectation that this would encourage competition in the banking and financial services industries. The president supported a new loan program for college students, an initiative popular with middle-class voters. As part of his proposal to reinvent government, Clinton cut the size of the federal work force. This, too, was a measure designed to appeal to middle-class taxpayers.

Despite these ideologically middle-of-the-road programs, a number of Clinton's other initiatives seemed calculated to please liberals. As part of his plan to reduce the nation's projected budget deficit, the president's 1992 and 1993 budgets called for tax increases, to be borne primarily by wealthy taxpayers. These were adopted in 1993. He also proposed a new tax on energy consumption—the so-called Btu tax (a tax based on the heat content of energy)—that was defeated in 1993. In an attempt to take the issue of public safety away from the Republicans, Clinton introduced his own anti-crime legislation, but buried increased social spending, under the rubric of "crime prevention," within the bill. He sup-

ported gun-control efforts, securing the passage of the Brady bill, which had
been debated in Congress for seven years. Clinton enraged social conservatives
and the religious Right by supporting efforts to end discrimination against gays
and lesbians in the military, and made race and gender diversity a major criterion
for federal appointments.

The most important proposal of Clinton's first two years was his health care
reform initiative, developed by a 500-person task force under the direction of
First Lady Hillary Rodham Clinton. The administration favored a form of "managed competition," in which the federal government would oversee the creation
of large groups of health care purchasers, who would contract with the health
maintenance organization that offered the most complete package of medical services at the lowest cost. Clinton's plan was supported by many liberals, although
some thought that the president's plan did not involve the government enough.
Conservatives and even moderates opposed Clinton's plan, fearing that it would
increase the cost and reduce the quality and availability of health care services to
middle- and upper-middle-class Americans.[4]

On the political front, Clinton proposed changes in campaign spending rules
to limit private contributions and to provide voluntary public funding for congressional campaigns. He signed the "Motor-Voter" bill allowing individuals to
register to vote by mail when renewing their drivers' licenses. And he proposed
reforming the Hatch Act, a law that has prohibited federal employees from taking
part in partisan political activities since 1938. Clinton also proposed a new set of
rules that would prohibit lobbyists from making financial contributions to, or
raising funds on behalf of, members of Congress, the president, and the vice president if they had lobbied these officials within the previous twelve months. The
president sought legislation stipulating that companies employing lobbyists be
prohibited from deducting lobbying costs from their federal taxes as legitimate
business expenses as well. These rules would, in effect, make it more difficult and
more costly for firms to employ lobbyists on behalf of their concerns.

Taken together, the elements of Clinton's program seemed to be a recipe for
expanding the power of the Democratic party in national politics. Clinton's economic package entailed substantial tax increases and cuts in military spending,
making additional revenues available for Democratic social programs and agencies
that had been starved for funding through twelve years of Republican rule. Although he called it deficit reduction, Clinton was actually proposing to step up
domestic spending. This would dramatically and definitively exorcise the legacy
of Ronald Reagan that had haunted Democrats in the 1980s and early 1990s.

Clinton's health care reform proposals promised to create an enormous new
set of agencies and institutions that would permit Democrats to expand substantially their influence over an area representing nearly 15 percent of the domestic
economy while simultaneously strengthening the attachment of important constituency groups to the Democratic party. Health care promised to do for the
Clintonites what Social Security had done for Franklin Roosevelt and his Democratic party in the 1930s: It would provide millions of voters with an incentive to

[4]Dan Balz, "Health Plan Was Albatross for Democrats: Big Government Labels Hurt Party, Polls Find,"
Washington Post, 18 November 1994, p. A1.

support the Democrats and give the Democratic party a new institutional base for managing the domestic economy.

Finally, Clinton's proposed changes in campaign spending rules would generally work to the advantage of liberal, public-interest groups and Democratic incumbents and against traditionally well-financed Republican candidates; the "Motor-Voter" Act could bring somewhat larger numbers of mainly Democratic poor and minority voters to the polls; and reform of the Hatch Act would permit the heavily Democratic federal civil service to play a larger role in the political process.[5]

Thus, the president made a bold effort to take advantage of his hard-won and precarious electoral victory by offering policy initiatives and creating programs that would ensure continuing Democratic control of the government. Adoption of his proposals would solidify the Democratic party's institutional base in the bureaucracies of the executive branch, while making it all the more difficult for Republicans to dislodge the Democrats in Congress through electoral methods. To his dismay, Clinton would soon find many of his efforts stymied in Congress by Republicans and even some Democrats.

Legislative Struggles

During his first year in office, President Clinton was able to claim some modest successes, most notably the passage of the North American Free Trade Agreement (NAFTA), which was won with the support of many Republicans in Congress. Indeed, Clinton had the highest success rate in Congress of any first-year president since Eisenhower in 1953; Clinton's "batting average," the frequency of presidential success in Congress on issues on which he had stated a clear position, was 86 percent, compared to Eisenhower's 89 percent. Although Clinton, like Eisenhower, enjoyed the advantage of having his own party in control of both the House and Senate, this could not have been the only reason for his success; both Kennedy's 1961 rating (81 percent) and Carter's 1977 rating (75.4 percent) were lower, despite Democratic control of Congress in those years, too.

Of course, statistical averages do not tell the whole story. Some of Clinton's legislative victories had been bottled up for years in a Democratic-controlled Congress that faced constant veto threats from Republican presidents Bush and Reagan; the "Motor Voter" bill, the Family Leave Act, and the Brady gun-control bill had all been opposed by President Bush. In these cases, Clinton's presence as a Democrat was more important than his legislative leadership. Yet, two bills that Clinton had put high on his agenda were passed partially as a result of his presidential leadership: NAFTA and a five-year, $500-billion deficit-reduction plan. Unwilling to credit these Republican-supported victories to a Democratic president, Senate minority leader Bob Dole was quick to point out that "Republicans made a difference."[6]

It should also be noted that Clinton's legislative failures involved three of the most important of his proposed new programs: economic policy, health care, and

[5]Chuck Alston, "Democrats Flex New Muscle with Trio of Election Bills: Some Republicans Say That 'Motor Voter,' Campaign Finance and Hatch Act Bills Add Up to Permanent Power Grab," *Congressional Quarterly Weekly Report*, 20 March 1993, pp. 643–45.

[6]George J. Church, "The Gridlock Breakers," *Time*, 6 December 1993, p. 32.

political reform. Despite their cooperation on the passage of NAFTA, most Republicans understood the threat that Clinton's programs posed to them and sought to block as much of the Clinton package as possible. In April 1993, a Republican filibuster in the Senate defeated Clinton's economic stimulus package, along with most of his plans for new federal social programs. All 43 Republican senators, joined by one Democrat (Senator Richard Shelby of Alabama), held firm against Clinton's proposal and prevented its consideration by the Senate. Clinton could muster only 56 of the 60 votes needed to end the filibuster. His campaign-finance reform proposals were finally defeated by Congress in October 1994, and although Congress passed the "Motor-Voter" legislation, it refused to approve funding for the program. Madison's ghost had returned with a vengeance.

Clinton's proposals also sparked opposition from a variety of interest groups that feared adverse economic or political consequences from the changes he advocated. The president's struggle to build support for his health care reform proposals illustrates the enormous role that special interests have come to play in American politics. Even before the contents of his reform package were fully known, campaigns were launched by various interests—public employee unions, groups of physicians, business organizations, the pharmaceutical industry, insurance companies, nursing groups, mental health professionals, and even chiropractors—all wanting to have a say about the plan.

Large insurance companies, including Prudential, Aetna, and Cigna, organized as the Alliance for Managed Competition and enthusiastically supported what was generally seen as the president's preferred health care option. Large insurers liked the idea of managed competition because, as envisioned by the president and first lady, it promised to give them virtual control of the nation's health care system at the expense of physicians and smaller insurance concerns.[7] Indeed, the major insurers had worked for years to shape the health care debate by their involvement in the Jackson Hole Group, which pioneered the notion of managed competition.[8]

Smaller insurance companies, not surprisingly, sought to resist this effort by the giants to put them out of business. Their lobby, the Health Insurance Association of America (HIAA), led by a former member of Congress, Willie Gradison, mounted a grassroots campaign against managed competition. The most memorable element of this effort was a $12-million series of thirty-second television spots featuring "Harry and Louise," actors depicting a middle-aged American couple who raise questions about President Clinton's health care plan. Harry and Louise proved so effective in creating public doubt about the plan that, at one point, the chairman of the House Ways and Means Committee felt compelled to make a number of concessions to the HIAA in exchange for its agreement to keep Harry and Louise off the air while his committee considered health care legislation.[9]

Similarly, pharmaceutical manufacturers sponsored an advertising campaign

[7]Robin Toner, "Lobbyists Scurry for a Place on the Health-Reform Train," *New York Times*, 20 March 1993, p. 1.

[8]Alissa J. Rubin, "Special Interests Stampede to Be Heard on Overhaul," *Congressional Quarterly Weekly Report*, 1 May 1993, pp. 1081–84.

[9]Michael Weisskopf, "Harry, Louise to Vacation During Hearings," *Washington Post*, 24 May 1994, p. 1.

designed to convince Americans that their own health could not be maintained without a healthy prescription drug industry.[10] Pharmaceutical industry representatives also lobbied congressional committees that were considering health care legislation. The industry's goal was to eliminate from the administration's proposal the requirement that drug companies rebate to the government a portion of their earnings from the federal Medicare program to help finance health care reform.

The most effective lobbying effort directed against the president's health care proposal was mounted by owners of small businesses. They objected to the chief mechanism through which Clinton proposed to finance the new health care system—the employer mandate—which would require employers to pay much of the cost of their employees' health care coverage. The National Federation of Independent Business (NFIB) organized meetings and community forums around the country, and its members began a relentless campaign of letters, calls, and faxes to committee members, arguing that small business would be ruined and the local economy destroyed by employer mandates. Lobbying efforts by the NFIB were among the most important factors leading to the defeat of comprehensive health care reform proposals in 1994.[11]

The administration denounced all these special-interest activities, and at one point, Clinton rejected a plea from the American Medical Association to be included in the health care reform planning process.[12] At the same time, however, the administration prepared its own public relations campaign, with funds raised by the Democratic National Committee, to sell health care reform to the public and to Congress. In response to HIAA's televised campaign against managed competition, the White House followed with its own series of thirty-second television parodies of "Harry and Louise."[13] Assuming that congressional Republicans would bitterly oppose his major effort to expand the Democratic party's political base and institutional power, Clinton recognized that such a campaign could be crucial.

In a similar vein, groups representing banking, energy, real estate, and farming interests mobilized to seek changes in portions of Clinton's economic program. Even lobbyists organized to lobby against the president's proposed changes in laws governing lobbying. In particular, they feared that Clinton's proposal to eliminate the tax deductibility of corporate lobbying expenses would lead business interests to reduce these activities. The American League of Lobbyists, a trade group representing this business, quickly mobilized its members to conduct a vigorous campaign to defeat the proposal. Still, one worried Washington lobbyist observed, "This seems so self-serving, you wonder who is going to listen to us anyway."[14]

[10]Howard Kurtz, "For Health Care Lobbies, a Major Ad Operation," *Washington Post*, 13 April 1993, p. D1.

[11]Neil A. Lewis, "Lobbying for Small Business Owners Puts Big Dent in Health Care," *New York Times*, 6 July 1994, p. 1.

[12]Robert Pear, "White House Shuns Bigger A.M.A. Voice in Health Changes," *New York Times*, 5 March 1993, p. 1.

[13]David S. Broder, "White House Takes on Harry and Louise," *Washington Post*, 8 July 1994, p. A11.

[14]Michael Weisskopf, "Lobbyists Rally around Their Own Cause: Clinton Move to Eliminate Tax Break Sparks Intense Hill Campaign," *Washington Post*, 14 May 1993, p. A16.

Partisan Antagonism The greatest challenges to Clinton came from Republican opponents trying to dig up scandals from the president's past. The first potential skeleton they found concerned the Whitewater affair, in which the president's critics charged that he and his wife had been guilty of a variety of conflicts of interest and financial improprieties while involved in a partnership with an Arkansas banker and real estate developer. A special prosecutor, Robert Fiske, was appointed to look into the charges, and Republicans demanded that congressional hearings on the issue be scheduled. Democrats opposed hearings, arguing that the Republicans merely sought to embarrass the administration. Finally, hearings were scheduled, but under very limited conditions that Democrats hoped would protect the president from any new, potentially embarrassing disclosures.

The president's critics also questioned the circumstances under which Mrs. Clinton had been able to earn a profit of more than $100,000 in a short period of time, through a series of speculative commodities trades. Critics noted that Mrs. Clinton, who had no experience in the commodities market, had been guided by an attorney for Tyson Foods, Inc., a huge, Arkansas-based poultry producer that stood to gain from the friendship of then-Governor Clinton. Although the White House denied any wrongdoing on the first lady's part, the charges produced at least the appearance of impropriety.

In yet another challenge to Clinton, a former Arkansas state employee, Paula Jones, charged that she had been propositioned and sexually harassed by then-Governor Clinton in a hotel room to which she had been led by an Arkansas state trooper. Jones had made no mention of the incident for many years, but was encouraged to come forward with her story by conservative groups who hoped to damage the president. Clinton denied the charges, but Jones filed a civil suit against the president. Clinton's defense team argued successfully that a president should not have to defend himself against civil lawsuits until after his term ended. Otherwise, the president's lawyers argued, the orderly process of government would be disrupted.

Factional Strife Clinton also faced strong opposition within his own party. Clinton had campaigned for office as a centrist, a "New Democrat," but to maintain the support of powerful liberal forces in the Democratic party, Clinton felt compelled to adopt a much more liberal stance on domestic social spending, as well as on gay rights, abortion, minority representation, and other causes championed by the liberal Democrats. Campaign promises such as welfare reform and the "middle-class tax cut," backed by centrists, were forgotten. In the eyes of the Clintonites, it was Carter's failure to reach out to the party's liberal wing after campaigning as a moderate that had led to the collapse of his presidency twelve years earlier. [15]

But perhaps they should have looked to a more recent presidency to find out how costly moving away from the center can be. A centrist himself, George Bush had felt compelled to try to maintain the allegiance of his party's conservative

[15]Fred Barnes, "Back to Basics," *New Republic*, 17 May 1993, pp. 16–18. See also Michael Kelly, "New Democrats Say Clinton Has Veered Left and Left Them," *New York Times*, 23 May 1993, p. 20, and Adam Clymer, "Single-Minded President," *New York Times*, 4 April 1993, p. 1.

wing by championing their views on abortion and other social issues. By moving to the right, of course, Bush alienated moderate Republicans. In a similar way, as Clinton sought to accommodate liberal forces, he ran the risk of losing the support of Democrats from other parts of the political spectrum. When liberals insisted that the president's health care reform package include a guarantee of funding for abortions for all women, conservatives vowed to oppose the entire plan.[16] Clinton's effort to end the military's ban on gay personnel also engendered intense opposition, both within the armed services and among conservative and even moderate Democrats. Senator Sam Nunn of Georgia, the powerful chair of the Senate Armed Services Committee, led this Democratic opposition. Similarly, Clinton's efforts to conciliate liberals by expanding domestic spending programs led to a revolt among conservative and moderate Democrats, who demanded the imposition of caps on the growth of entitlement programs such as Medicare.[17] Factional struggles within the Democratic party also broke out over labor policy.[18] And in mid-May 1993, conservative Democrats in the House of Representatives nearly refused to support the president's economic program. Only under enormous pressure from the House leadership did most Democrats finally back the president. With the passage of the program by a slim three-vote margin,[19] the administration survived what some observers characterized as a "near-death experience."

Chastened by these events, Clinton moved to respond to the criticisms of Democratic moderates and conservatives. He revived discussion of the middle-class tax cut and signalled a willingness to compromise with Democratic conservatives on taxes and spending. Nevertheless, the president's economic program was delayed for several weeks in the Senate, where senators from energy-producing states, led by Oklahoma Democrat David Boren, objected to Clinton's proposed Btu tax.

The Senate's Democratic leadership became increasingly concerned that the administration's difficulties, if unchecked, would lead to a total collapse and might even hurt Democratic senators and House members up for re-election in 1994.[20] A Republican landslide in the June 1993 special election to replace Texas Senator Lloyd Bentsen (who was appointed treasury secretary) heightened these fears. To prevent a complete disaster, Democratic leaders in the Senate took charge of the budget package in the finance committee, substituting a higher gasoline sales tax for the Btu tax, cutting Medicare spending, and making a number of other changes. During the 1992 campaign, Clinton had vehemently opposed any suggestion of raising the gasoline tax. Senate leaders suggested that the president confine himself to enunciating broad principles while leaving it to Congress to develop the "details" of legislation.[21]

[16]Dana Priest, "Health Plan Threatened by Abortion Coverage," *Washington Post*, 19 May 1993, p. 1.

[17]Eric Pianin, "Hill Democrats Press for Entitlement Caps," *Washington Post*, 8 May 1993, p. 1.

[18]Mickey Kaus, "Bad Wagner," *New Republic*, 7 June 1993, p. 6.

[19]See Jon Healey, "Clinton Struggles with Hill but Still Gets His Way," *Congressional Quarterly Weekly Report*, 29 May 1993, pp. 1335–36.

[20]David Broder, "Democrats Worrying: Clinton's Problems Raise Fears for 1994," *Washington Post*, 9 June 1993, p. 1.

[21]Ann Devroy and Eric Pianin, "Clinton Yields on Energy Tax," *Washington Post*, 9 June 1993, p. 1.

Finally, in August 1993, a budget was enacted by Congress and signed into law by the president. This budget, however, bore little resemblance to Clinton's initial proposals. Congressional opponents forced Clinton to abandon the bulk of his package of social and economic "investments." The comprehensive new energy tax proposed by the president was converted into a trivial increase in the gasoline tax. One journalist, sympathetic to Clinton's original goals, called the budget that emerged from Congress a "far cry" from Clinton's campaign promises and hardly a long-term solution to the nation's problems.[22] Because of defections by conservative Democrats, the president's victory margin on the budget was razor thin. Clinton won in the House by merely two votes, 218 to 216. In the Senate, Vice President Gore was forced to cast a tie-breaking vote to give the Clinton budget a 51-to-50 edge.

In addition to factional opposition, Clinton's efforts were hampered by the fact that many congressional Democrats have become "soloists," willing to give the administration their support only in exchange for some set of tangible benefits for themselves and the interests they represent. In the absence of party organizations and mechanisms for enforcing party discipline, there is little to prevent legislators from demanding what amounts to immediate political payoffs in exchange for their support on important pieces of legislation. The result is that all legislation effectively becomes special-interest legislation, filled with loopholes and benefits written to garner the support of a variety of different interests and their congressional representatives.

For example, the 1993 budget contains provisions requiring that cigarettes manufactured in the United States contain 75 percent domestically grown tobacco. This provision was inserted at the behest of Senator Wendell Ford of Kentucky for the benefit of his state's tobacco farmers. Similarly, Democratic Representative James Bilbray of Nevada agreed to support the budget only after securing the addition of a tax credit designed to offset the Social Security taxes paid by restaurant owners—an important constituency group in his district—on their employees' tips. Texas Democrat Solomon Ortiz traded his support for the president's budget for an enlarged share of defense conversion funds for his district. The list goes on and on.[23] No wonder that distinguished columnist David Broder called the resulting budget a "pastiche of conflicting goals."[24] One Clinton administration official conceded that because the budget was "driven by politics not policy," it was "not the greatest package ever."[25]

Clinton's political appointment came under repeated attack. Seeking to placate conservative and moderate Democrats, Clinton withdrew his nomination of Lani Guinier, an African American law professor, to head the civil rights division of the Justice Department. Conservatives had strongly opposed the Guinier nomination, saying she would use her position to promote racial quotas in employment and elsewhere. Dubbing Guinier a "quota queen," critics complained that her

[22]David Broder, "Some Victory," *Washington Post*, 10 August 1993, p. A15.

[23]David Rogers and John Harwood, "No Reasonable Offer Refused as Administration Bargained to Nail Down Deficit Package in House," *Wall Street Journal*, 6 August 1993, p. A12.

[24]Broder, "Some Victory."

[25]Hobart Rowan, "It's Not Much of a Budget," *Washington Post*, 12 August 1993, p. A27.

scholarly writings called for novel forms of proportional representation and minority veto powers that would increase the political influence of the black community only at the expense of democratic principles.[26]

Clinton's decision to withdraw the nomination was based on a political calculation similar to one that he had made during the 1992 campaign. The president concluded that, although they would be angered by his actions, African Americans and their liberal political allies ultimately would have no choice but to continue to support his administration. If he continued to alienate conservative Democrats, on the other hand, Clinton would undermine his chances of winning their approval for his economic, health care, and political reform proposals. Clinton was especially concerned about the views of the Southern Democratic senators whose backing he desperately needed to enact his major programs. Southern Democrats rely heavily upon the support of black voters, who account for more than half the Democratic vote in some Southern states. However, these senators must also win the votes of a reasonable number of conservative white voters. To maintain their delicate biracial coalitions, the Southern Democrats generally adopt a posture of social liberalism and fiscal conservatism—the former to win the favor of African Americans and the latter to placate whites—and seek to avoid dealing with divisive racial issues.[27] For the Southern Democrats, the Guinier nomination represented a major political threat. If they opposed Guinier, their black constituents would be outraged. If they supported Guinier, they would alienate white voters. The Southerners were furious that Clinton would put them in such a dangerous position and demanded that the president withdraw the nomination.

In the end, the president's handling of the Guinier nomination proved divisive and costly. Clinton's efforts to satisfy moderates and conservatives deeply offended liberal Democrats, while doing little to placate the party's other wing. Civil rights leaders denounced the president for failing to allow Guinier an opportunity to present her case to the Senate Judiciary Committee during confirmation hearings. Representative Kweisi Mfume, head of the Congressional Black Caucus, said angrily, "Some people who worked to put Bill Clinton in office, who took to heart his pledge to bring about change, to some extent, feel betrayed." Conservatives, for their part, expressed disdain for the president's "waffling," and condemned him as an individual whose "only core principle is to bend to the strongest political force."[28]

The Media   In addition to the problems he faced from interest-group opposition, partisan antagonism, and factional struggle in his own party, Clinton quickly found himself under attack from the national news media. Many journalists had implicitly or explicitly supported Clinton during the 1992 campaign. As has often been noted, many of America's most prominent journalists tend to identify themselves as liberal Democrats.[29] Moreover, since the Vietnam War, there has

[26]Clint Bolick, "The Legal Philosophy that Produced Lani Guinier," *Wall Street Journal*, 2 June 1993, p. A15.

[27]See Donald Beachler, "The South and Divided Government," unpublished doctoral thesis, Cornell University, 1992.

[28]Paul A. Gigot, "Guinier is Going, No, She's Staying, No, Going . . . ," *Wall Street Journal*, 4 June 1993, p. A14.

[29]Michael Kinsley, "Bias and Baloney," *New Republic*, 14 December 1992, p. 6.

been a confluence of interests between segments of the media and liberal political forces in the United States. As a result of these two factors, much of the national media had been more critical of George Bush than of Bill Clinton during the campaign. Indeed, the media gave relatively little attention to a potentially damaging tape recording of a conversation purported to be between Clinton and Gennifer Flowers, a woman with whom he had been accused of having an affair.[30] In addition, the national media generally rebuffed George Bush's efforts to focus the campaign on Clinton's "character," and it supported Clinton's assertion that Bush's attacks on his draft record were attempts to divert public attention from the "real" issues.

During his first two months in office, President Clinton seemed to have considerable media support. After the president's initial budget proposals were accepted by Congress, he was hailed as a political genius. One front page *Washington Post* story described the capital as "dazzled" by Clinton's acumen and approvingly quoted a Republican strategist who called Clinton "as formidable a political figure as I've seen in my lifetime."[31]

A few weeks later, however, the media had begun to adopt a considerably more critical stance. In the wake of the Republican senatorial filibuster that defeated Clinton's proposed economic stimulus package, many commentators concluded that Clinton was inept after all. After his first one hundred days in office, the president was accused of having lost his focus, of being disorganized, of trying to do too many things at once. Suddenly, the capital was said to be more doubtful than dazzled.[32] Not surprisingly, the president was reported to distrust and dislike the Washington press.[33]

Why did the president's relationship with the national media sour so quickly? First, the U.S. news media's techniques of investigating and criticizing—adversarial journalism—enhance the power and status of the media relative to other American political and social institutions. For this reason, any administration can expect a certain amount of critical coverage. For example, during the 1992 campaign and the early days of the Clinton presidency, the major media gave little attention to the Whitewater story or to the various rumors and allegations that had circulated about Clinton, despite the attention being paid to these issues by the conservative media. But eventually, the mainstream media, afraid of missing important stories, began their own probes. In due course, the investigative instincts of the national media overcame any sympathy reporters felt for a Democratic president. To have failed to investigate and reveal would have amounted to a media abdication from the position of power they had won over the past quarter-century. Once their investigative energies were revived, the mainstream media dug into the stories, cheerfully reporting even the most outrageous rumors and allegations. Most newspapers, for example, gave at least some credence to the

[30]See Mickey Kaus, "Tribal Hatred," *New Republic*, 21 June 1993, p. 4.

[31]David Von Drehle, "Beginner's Luck or President's Prowess? Dazzled Capital Wonders if Clinton Can Keep Lighting Up the Board," *Washington Post*, 26 March 1993, p. A1.

[32]See, for example, Thomas B. Edsall, "Clinton Loses Focus—and Time," *Washington Post*, 2 May 1993, p. C1.

[33]Jeffrey Birnbaum, "Resentful of Negative Coverage, Clinton Spurns the Media, but He May Need to Woo Them Back," *Wall Street Journal*, 15 April 1993, p. A16.

since-debunked rumor that former White House counsel Vincent Foster had not committed suicide, but instead had been murdered as part of some complex presidential plot.[34]

The second reason that the president's relationship with the press soured is that Clinton and members of his staff responded to media criticism in ways that were guaranteed to antagonize journalists and generate even more hostility. To avoid questions, the president spurned press conferences in favor of "town meetings" with the public. Members of his staff observed that the president did not need the media and could reach "over their heads" to the American public. At the same time, large sections of the White House press office, and thus the people who work there, were declared "off-limits" to reporters, who resented what they saw as another effort to block their access to legitimate news.

Some members of the media reacted to the administration's clumsy efforts to thwart them by filing stories that presented the president in an unfavorable light. Clinton's expensive haircut while Air Force One was parked at the Los Angeles airport was turned into a front-page story about presidential arrogance. The firing of members of the White House travel office became "Travelgate," a banner headline account of presidential cronyism and misuse of power. The media certainly did not imagine these events. They were real. The point is, however, that at least partly because the president and his staff had antagonized reporters, the same media that had previously ignored Gennifer Flowers and played down the character issue were now prepared to put a different slant on the Clinton story.

During his first weeks in office, Clinton was permitted a measure of "spin control"—that is, he was allowed to put his own gloss on news stories. For example, he was allowed to define his social service and public works programs as "investments"; he was allowed to call his economic program—which raised spending more than taxes—a "deficit reduction" effort; he was permitted to define the nation's health care problems as a "crisis"; he was permitted to define rather minor administrative changes as a "reinvention" of government. As media antagonism toward the administration grew, however, the media resolved to put this White House "spinning" to a stop. "They [the Clinton administration] don't know the difference between truth and lies," one White House reporter complained.[35] Members of the media now would be certain to teach the White House all it needed to know about this distinction—at least as reporters saw it.

Clinton might also have hoped he could smooth the media's ruffled feathers through the appointment of David Gergen, a successful Republican "spin doctor," to the White House staff. Once in place, Gergen sought to develop a better relationship with the national media. He scheduled a White House cook-out for reporters, removed restrictions on media access to presidential press aides, and sought to schedule several traditional presidential press conferences to give journalists the opportunity they had been demanding to question the president.[36]

But the first of these news conferences, on June 14, 1993, ended rather badly.

[34]Howard Kurtz, "The Media and the Fiske Report: Critics Say Press Made Rush to Judgment About Foster Suicide," *Washington Post*, 3 July 1994, p. A4.

[35]Quoted in Kaus, "Tribal Hatred."

[36]See Gwen Ifill, "Clinton, in Prime Time, Spurned by Two Networks," *New York Times*, 18 June 1993, p. A18.

BOX 1
The One-Question News Conference

After remarks by Supreme Court nominee Ruth Bader Ginsburg, President Clinton took a question from Brit Hume of ABC News. The news conference opened and closed with this exchange:

Q: "Mr. President, the result of the Guinier nomination, sir, and your apparent focus on Judge Breyer, and your turn, late it seems, to Judge Ginsburg may have created an impression, perhaps unfair, of a certain zigzag quality in the decision-making process here. I wonder, sir, if you could kind of walk us through it and perhaps disabuse us of any notion we might have along those lines. Thank you."

A: "I have long since given up the thought that I could disabuse some of you of turning any substantive decision into anything but a political process. How you could ask a question like that after the statement she just made is beyond me.
"Goodbye. Thank you."

Sources: Cable News Network; reprinted from *Washington Post*, 15 June 1993, p. A13.

Clinton had just nominated Ruth Bader Ginsburg to the U.S. Supreme Court, filling the vacancy created by Justice Byron White's pending retirement. Ginsburg was nominated after the White House had floated several other names, and then given every impression that the nominee was to be another federal judge, Stephen Breyer. Brit Hume of ABC News was the first reporter recognized by the president. Hume asked a question that seemed to Clinton to imply criticism of the selection process used to fill the Court seat. The president gave an angry response and stalked off, refusing to take any more questions (see Box 1).[37]

What came to be known as the "one-question news conference" drew angry responses from the national media. The next day, the nation's most influential newspapers, the *New York Times* and the *Washington Post*, both published editorials praising Judge Ginsburg but sharply criticizing the White House for its selection process.[38] The *Times* castigated the president for "an intemperate response to a reporter's question about his erratic selection process."[39] And the *Post*, in its news coverage, ridiculed the selection process as erratic and ultimately based on the

[37]Howard Kurtz, "One Question Too Many for Clinton," *Washington Post*, 15 June 1993, p. A13.

[38]See "Mr. Clinton Picks a Justice," *New York Times*, 15 June 1993, p. A26, and "Judge Ginsburg's Nomination . . . and Getting There," *Washington Post*, 15 June 1993, p. A20.

[39]"Mr. Clinton Picks a Justice."

president's personal rapport with the nominee—"personal karma," the *Post* called it—rather than reasoned judgment.[40]

Later in the week, the White House scheduled a prime time press conference, hoping to use reporters' questions to review the Clinton administration's achievements. Presidential press secretary Dee Dee Myers called it "an opportunity to give the American people a progress report." Two of the national networks, however, refused to carry it. Network executives saw the conference as simply another effort by David Gergen to manipulate the news.[41]

Eventually, however, Gergen's strategy paid off; by mid-1994, the press had begun to moderate its attacks upon Clinton. Indeed, a number of journalists began to ask whether they and their colleagues had not been too harsh in their criticisms. By this time, however, the damage had already been done. Clinton had been publicly depicted as boorish, arrogant, and unfeeling—hardly qualities likely to endear him to the electorate.

While the liberal national journalists began to feel sorry for Clinton and to tone down their attacks, another set of reporters and commentators was just beginning to take aim at the president. Over the past several years a conservative media complex has emerged in opposition to the liberal media. This complex includes two major newspapers, the *Wall Street Journal* and the *Washington Times*, several magazines such as the *American Spectator*, and a number of conservative radio and television talk programs.

Conservative religious leaders like Rev. Jerry Falwell and Pat Robertson, leader of the Christian Coalition, have used their television shows to attack the president's programs and to mount biting personal attacks on both Clinton and his wife. For example, a videotape promoted by Falwell accuses Clinton of arranging for the murder of an Arkansas investigator who allegedly had evidence of the president's sexual misconduct. Other conservative groups not associated with the religious Right have also launched sharp assaults against the president. Nationally syndicated talk-show host Rush Limbaugh is a constant critic of the administration. Floyd Brown, leader of Citizens United, a group with 40 employees and a $3-million annual budget, attacks Clinton on a daily radio show and faxes anti-Clinton news bulletins to more than 1,200 journalists and talk-show hosts.

The emergence of this complex has meant that liberal policies and politicians are virtually certain to come under attack even when the "liberal media" are sympathetic to them. For example, the Whitewater affair and the charges by Paula Jones of sexual harassment were first publicized by the conservative press. In due course, as we saw earlier, the liberal media probably gave the Whitewater and Jones charges as much play as the conservative media, often with just as little regard for hard evidence.

Attacks by the media and by Clinton's Republican opponents were extremely effective. Substantial segments of the public formed images of the president as an individual lacking scruples and moral standards. These attacks are partially responsible for the drop in Clinton's standing in public opinion polls in 1994 despite

[40]See Ann Devroy and Ruth Marcus, "After 87 Days, Tortuous Selection Process Came Down to Karma," *Washington Post*, 15 June 1993, p. A11.

[41]Ifill, "Clinton, in Prime Time."

the strong performance of the American economy in that same year. Usually, presidential popularity and the nation's economic performance are closely linked. Clinton had become an object of such opprobrium that many Americans were unwilling to credit him with any positive developments.

By June 1994, Clinton had become so angry about the tenor of media coverage of his administration that he lashed out at the media. Previous presidents have done the same. Richard Nixon, for example, sent his vice president, Spiro Agnew, to attack broadcasters as "nattering nabobs of negativism." But usually, the last word in such debates belongs to the press. President Clinton noted in his critical comments about Rush Limbaugh that the radio host would later have three hours "to say whatever he wants," but that the American people would have no way to know whether what Limbaugh said was true. During his program that same afternoon, Limbaugh replied, "There is no need for a truth detector. I am the truth detector."[42] Subsequently, Clinton was forced to adopt a more conciliatory tone toward the press.

White House Blunders   Finally, Clinton's efforts to maintain the support of his own party, defeat the Republicans, overcome interest-group opposition, and maintain favorable media coverage—necessary conditions for presidential power—were undermined by a series of blunders and miscues by members of the White House staff and the president himself. For example, in the Travelgate affair, Clinton aides fired members of the White House staff who had been making travel arrangements for Washington journalists for years. It seemed that they had been fired in order to clear the way for the appointment of a Clinton relative to head the office. When fired staffers complained to their media friends, Clinton aides claimed that the firings had been sparked by possible fraud under investigation by the FBI. It quickly became clear that the FBI had been manipulated and possibly misused by the White House in order to prompt an investigation of the travel office.[43] The entire matter smacked of misjudgment and ineptitude.

In a similar vein, Clinton's handling of the Guinier case indicated inattention and misjudgment on the part of staffers and the president himself. Apparently, no one in the White House realized that Guinier's nomination might create a political firestorm. By the time the president and his staff became aware of the problem, Clinton found himself having to decide whether to anger his liberal allies or offend the moderates and conservatives whose backing he needed—a no-win situation. The fault, to paraphrase Cassius, was not only in Clinton's stars.

Two years of Republican attacks, factionalism among Democrats in Congress, unfavorable media coverage, and seeming ineptitude in the White House caused Clinton's public approval ratings to plummet and encouraged congressional Republicans to refuse to make even token efforts to cooperate with the president. As the 1994 midterm Congressional elections approached, many Democrats dis-

[42]Douglas Jehl, "Clinton Calls Show to Assail Press, Falwell and Limbaugh," *New York Times*, 25 June 1994, p. 1.

[43]Michael K. Frisby, "Travel Office Trouble Casts a Shadow on Clinton, the Press and Seven Staffers," *Wall Street Journal*, 24 May 1993, p. A5. See also Meg Greenfield, "The 'Moi?' Defense," *Washington Post*, 31 May 1993, p. A19.

tanced themselves from the president, fearful that his unpopularity would work against them at the polls. Indeed, many Democratic candidates seemed to be running as much against the president as against their Republican opponents. Meanwhile, Republicans in Congress stalled or quashed piece after piece of legislation, particularly the various health care reform proposals. By the end of the summer of 1994, it looked as though the Democratic administration and the Democratic Congress couldn't get anything done. The results of the 1994 election showed that much of the country agreed.

THE 1994 ELECTION AND BEYOND

After two years of legislative struggle, the Clinton administration and the Democratic party suffered a stunning defeat in the November 1994 election. For the first time since 1946, Republicans won simultaneous control of both houses of Congress, and were in a position to block President Clinton's legislative efforts and to promote their own policy agenda.

In Senate races, the Republicans gained eight seats to achieve a 52-to-48 majority. Immediately after the election, Alabama Senator Richard Shelby, a conservative Democrat who frequently voted with the Republicans, announced that he was formally joining the GOP. His move gave the Republicans 53 votes in the upper chamber. In House races, the Republicans gained an astonishing 52 seats to win a 230-to-204 majority (one House seat is held by an Independent). Gaining control of the House was a significant achievement for the Republican party, for although it had controlled the Senate as recently as 1986, the House of Representatives had been a Democratic bastion since 1954.

Republicans also posted a net gain of eleven governorships and won control of fifteen additional chambers in state legislatures. A number of the Democratic party's leading figures were defeated, including Governor Mario Cuomo of New York, former House Ways and Means Committee chair Dan Rostenkowski of Illinois, House Judiciary Committee chair Jack Brooks of Texas, three-term Senator Jim Sasser of Tennessee and, most shocking of all, Speaker of the House Thomas Foley of Washington. Foley became the first sitting Speaker to be defeated for re-election to his own congressional seat since 1860. All told, 34 incumbent Democratic representatives, 3 incumbent Democratic senators, and 4 incumbent Democratic governors went down to defeat. On the Republican side, in contrast, not one of the 10 incumbent senators, 15 incumbent governors, or 155 incumbent House members seeking re-election was defeated. The South, which had voted Republican in presidential elections for twenty years, now seemed to have turned to the GOP at the congressional level as well. Republicans posted gains among nearly all groups in the populace, with white male voters, in particular, switching to the GOP in large numbers. The nation's electoral map had been substantially altered overnight (see Figure 1). Interest in the hard-fought race had even produced a slight increase in voter turnout, *albeit* to a still-abysmal 39 percent.

The 1994 election seemed to be a nationwide repudiation of the Democratic

FIGURE 1
1994 Races for the Senate

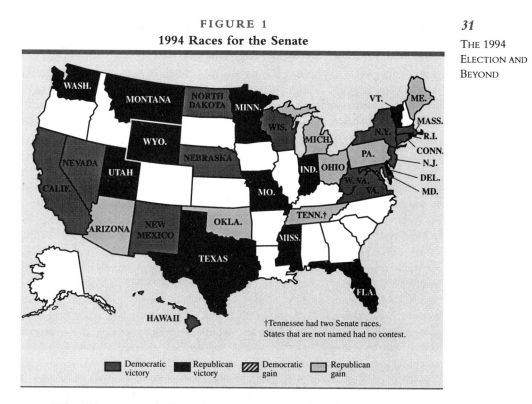

†Tennessee had two Senate races.
States that are not named had no contest.

Democratic victory | Republican victory | Democratic gain | Republican gain

party. Why did this occur? Why after two years had Clinton's bright beginnings and promises of "change" ended in electoral disaster? What would the election mean for the Democratic and Republican parties and for the nation?

The Republican Strategy

During the two years that Republicans had been attacking the president, they had also launched a major effort to win control of Congress. This effort had three elements. The first, spearheaded by Representative Newt Gingrich, actually began during the late 1980s with an attempt to discredit the Democratic party's congressional leadership. In 1989, Gingrich initiated a series of charges of financial impropriety that led to the resignations of Democratic House Speaker Jim Wright and House Democratic Whip Tony Coelho. In 1991, Gingrich and his allies launched attacks upon the operation of the House bank and post office that revealed that some House members were misusing these institutions for personal financial gain. Though some Republicans were affected by the ensuing scandals, most of the onus fell on the Democratic leadership of the House, which, indeed, was ultimately responsible for the operations of the chamber.

The banking and post office exposés helped to undermine public confidence in the Congress and its leadership. The problem was exacerbated when evidence was revealed suggesting that Representative Dan Rostenkowski, the powerful Democratic chair of the House Ways and Means Committee, had used his access to the House post office for personal advantage. Rostenkowski was indicted on federal criminal charges and forced to step down from his committee chairman-ship. By 1994, Gingrich, who had in the meantime become minority whip and was in line to become Republican leader after the 1994 election, had succeeded in depicting the Democratic congressional leadership as a venal group out of touch with the needs of ordinary citizens. Such a leadership, and the Congress it led, might be vulnerable in an election.

The second element in the effort to win control of Congress was the full-scale mobilization of the religious and social conservatives whom Republicans had been courting for a number of years. As Republican strategists had long hoped, by 1994 these groups were organized into the Christian Coalition, which provided committed activists and volunteers for Republican congressional and local campaigns throughout the nation, particularly in the South.

At last the Republicans had an infantry force to match the liberal activists mobilized by their Democratic foes. If anything, the fervor of the Republican infantry exceeded that of the Democrats. To be sure, Republicans like Virginia senatorial candidate Ollie North, seen by voters as too closely associated with the Christian Right, often were unsuccessful. However, Christian Coalition activists played a role in many races, including ones in which Republican candidates were not overly identified with the religious Right. One post-election study suggested that more than 60 percent of the over 600 candidates supported by the Christian Right were successful in state, local, and congressional races in 1994.[44] The efforts of conservative Republican activists to bring voters to the polls is one major reason that turnout among Republicans exceeded Democratic turnout in a midterm election for the first time since 1970. This increased turnout was especially marked in the South, where the Christian Coalition was most active. In many congressional districts, Christian Coalition efforts on behalf of the Republicans were augmented by grassroots campaigns launched by the National Rifle Association (NRA) and the National Federation of Independent Business (NFIB). The NRA had been outraged by Democratic support for gun control legislation, while the NFIB had been energized by its campaign against employer mandates in the failed Clinton health care reform initiative. Both groups are well organized at the local level and were able to mobilize their members across the country to participate in congressional races.

Thus by 1994, Republicans had finally found a way to nationalize congressional and local races. Using the hundreds of "talk programs" that had been launched by local radio and television stations during the 1990s, the Republicans were able to bring national political issues and ideologies into the local community or congressional district. These programs are inexpensive to produce and popular with large groups of listeners and viewers. Often their hosts seek to link local politicians to national stories and to inform audiences of the positions on national political issues taken by their representatives. Talk radio and talk television programs, for example, played an important role in informing audiences about the role of their own representatives in the House banking and post office scandals.

[44]Richard L. Burke, "Religious-Right Candidates Gain as GOP Turnout Rises," *New York Times*, 12 November 1994, p. 10.

Although many of the hosts of these programs are politically conservative, not all take right-wing positions. In fact, during the 1992 presidential campaign many talk-show hosts supported Clinton. By bringing national issues into local races, however, these programs made it more difficult for congressional and local Democratic candidates to insulate themselves from the issues and ideologies that, for thirty years, have handicapped the Democratic party at the presidential level. This new media format made it less likely that a congressional district that voted Republican at the presidential level would also keep its Democratic congressional representative in office, a change that boded ill for Democrats, especially in the South.

The 104th Congress: Republicans in Power

All these factors produced the Democratic debacle of November 1994. For the first time in nearly half a century, the Republicans would control both houses of Congress. Yet what would this mean? What would the Republicans do with their new-found power? American history suggests that very little can be inferred from election results. What matters is what the victors do with their power once they have acquired it. Franklin Roosevelt made the Democrats the nation's majority party for fifty years not because he won the 1932 election, but rather because of the programs he crafted after coming to power. Whether the 1994 election turns out to be significant is a function of what the Republicans do, now that they are in power.

Some clues about GOP plans began to emerge even before the election. In September 1994, Newt Gingrich had persuaded nearly all Republican congressional candidates to sign a "Contract with America." The contract, which Republicans pledged to support if they won control of Congress, called for a variety of tax cuts as well as such popular political reforms as term limits and a balanced budget amendment (see Box 2). The contract was part of the GOP's effort to nationalize the election, as well as a first step by the Republican leadership to impose party discipline on their new troops. New Republican members of Congress who failed to follow the leadership's dictates could be accused of breaking their pledge to the American people.

At the same time that he was compelling Republicans to sign this contract, Gingrich told a group of lobbyists that after Republicans took control of Congress, the GOP would launch legislative investigations to look into wrong-doing in the executive branch. Just as Democratic congresses had used their power to investigate Republican presidents, so a Republican Congress would use its power to investigate the conduct of the Clinton presidency.

Prior to the opening of the 104th Congress, House Republicans elected Newt Gingrich to serve as Speaker. Richard Armey of Texas, a close Gingrich ally, was elected majority leader and Tom DeLay, also of Texas, was elected majority whip. Gingrich and Armey are both very conservative and hope to use their leadership positions to bring about major changes in the direction of American government.

House Democrats elected Richard Gephardt of Missouri, the former majority leader, to the post of minority leader. David Bonior of Michigan was re-elected

BOX 2
Republican "Contract with America"

10 bills to be considered during the first 100 days of a Republican-led 104th Congress	
Fiscal Responsibility Act	Would propose a constitutional amendment requiring the president to submit, and the Congress to pass, a balanced federal budget for each fiscal year; and would give the president a line-item veto over any specific budgetary provision in a bill passed by Congress.
Taking Back Our Streets Act	Would place limits on federal and state *habeas corpus* appeals; establish mandatory minimum sentences for those convicted of drug-related or violent crimes while using a gun; and rescind recently passed crime-prevention programs and replace them with block grants for local law-enforcement programs.
Personal Responsibility Act	Would limit eligibility for the federal Aid to Families with Dependent Children (AFDC) program; deny AFDC benefits to teenage mothers; impose work requirements for those receiving AFDC benefits; and transfer much of the responsibility for social welfare programs to the states.
Family Reinforcement Act	Would grant tax credits for adoption and for care of elderly dependents.
American Dream Restoration Act	Would grant tax credits for families with children and expand uses for Individual Retirement Accounts (IRAs).
National Security Restoration Act	Would restrict participation of U.S. forces in United Nations peacekeeping activities; subject all funding for and participation in U.N. peacekeeping activities to congressional approval; and reinstate development of "Star Wars" anti-ballistic-missile defense system and other such systems.
Senior Citizens' Equity Act	Would double the income level beyond which Social Security benefits are reduced; reduce taxes on upper-income recipients of Social Security; and create tax benefits for the purchase of private long-term health care insurance.
Job Creation and Wage Enhancement Act	Would cut the capital gains tax; increase the estate tax exemption; and impose additional requirements for and restrictions on federal regulation.
Common Sense Legal Reforms Act	Would require the loser to pay the legal expenses of the winner in lawsuits filed in federal courts; and reform product liability laws.
Citizen Legislature Act	Would propose a constitutional amendment to limit terms of senators and representatives to 12 years.

Source: House Republican Conference, *Legislative Digest*, 27 September 1994.

BOX 3
Party Leadership in the 104th Congress

The Senate	
Republican Leadership	*Majority Leader:* Robert Dole (KS)
	Majority Whip: Trent Lott (MS)
	Chief Deputy Whip: Judd Gregg (NH)
	Republican Senatorial Committee Chair: Alphonse D'Amato (NY)
	Republican Conference Chair: Thad Cochran (MS)
	Republican Conference Secretary: Connie Mack (FL)
	Republican Policy Committee Chair: Don Nickles (OK)
Democratic Leadership	*Minority Leader:* Tom Daschle (SD)
	Minority Whip: Wendell Ford (KY)
	Chief Deputy Whip: John Breaux (LA)
	Democratic Conference Secretary: Barbara Mikulski (MD)
	Democratic Policy Committee Chair: Harry Reid (NV)
	Democratic Steering Committee Chair: John Kerry (MA)

The House	
Republican Leadership	*Speaker:* Newt Gingrich (GA)
	Majority Leader: Richard Armey (TX)
	Majority Whip: Tom DeLay (TX)
	Republican Conference Chair: John Boehner (OH)
	Republican Conference Vice Chair: Susan Molinari (NY)
	Republican Conference Secretary: Barbara Vucanovich (NV)
	Republican Policy Committee Chair: Christopher Cox (CA)
Democratic Leadership	*Minority Leader:* Richard Gephardt (MO)
	Minority Whip: David Bonior (MI)
	Democratic Caucus Chair: Vic Fazio (CA)
	Democratic Caucus Vice Chair: Barbara Kennelly (CT)
	Democratic Steering Committee Co-Chair: Steny Hoyer (MD)

Democratic whip. The re-election of the Democratic party's established liberal leadership, despite the drubbing at the polls in 1994, displeased some conservative Democrats who saw it as a sign that the party had not learned from its electoral defeat.[45] Box 3 identifies the Democratic and Republican leaders of the 104th Congress.

During the first days of the 104th Congress, Gingrich moved quickly to consolidate his power and put forth his initial legislative agenda. Gingrich's first move was to reorganize the House in a way that would eradicate any vestiges of Democratic influence, streamline the chamber's operations, and significantly expand the power of the Speaker.[46] The new Speaker showed little inclination to

---

[45]Donna Cassata, "Conservatives' Pleas Go Unheeded as Democrats Keep Old Guard," *Congressional Quarterly Weekly Report*, 3 December 1994, pp. 3439–40.

[46]For discussions of the reforms mandated by the Republican leadership of the 104th Congress, see David S. Cloud, "GOP's Housecleaning Sweep Changes Rules, Cuts Groups," *Congressional Quarterly Weekly Report*, 10 December 1994, pp. 3487–89; Mary Jacoby, "New GOP Rules Lock in Power," *Roll Call*, 8 December 1994, p. 1; John B. Judis, "House Repairs," *Washington Post*, 18 December 1994, p. C1.

compromise with the Democrats, and began his term by placing strict limits on Democratic representation on major House committees. In the Senate, by contrast, Majority Leader Robert Dole sought to avoid picking fights with the Democrats.

Gingrich began his "house cleaning" by breaching the time-honored seniority rule and appointing committee chairs who were likely to be energetic and loyal. At Gingrich's behest, the Republican leadership selected Henry Hyde of Illinois rather than the more senior committee Republican, Carlos Moorhead of California, to chair the House Judiciary Committee. Similarly, Gingrich named the fifth-ranking Republican on the House Appropriations Committee, Bob Livingston of Louisiana, to chair that important panel. Thomas Bliley of Virginia, the second-ranking Republican on the Energy and Commerce Committee (renamed Commerce) was given the chair over the most senior GOP member. In addition, three freshmen, Tom Davis (VA), David McIntosh (IN), and Linda Smith (WA), were slated to head congressional subcommittees.[47] In each of these cases, Republican leaders were determined to appoint an active committee chair who would push hard for the leadership's program, even if that meant violating tradition.

It remains to be seen whether these departures from seniority mark a turning point in the history of the congressional committee system. It is more likely that the seniority system will gradually reassert itself. Use of the principle of seniority is one of the ways that the congressional parties seek to avoid bitter and divisive internal struggles for power. Given the difficulties of maintaining even a modicum of party unity, it seems unlikely that the House Republicans will abandon the seniority system for long.

In addition to overriding seniority in their appointment of committee chairs, Gingrich and the Republican leaders moved to partially reorganize the committee system itself. Three House committees—Post Office, District of Columbia, and Merchant Marine and Fisheries—were eliminated and their functions transferred to other committees. Nominally, these committees were eliminated to streamline House operations. Political considerations also played a role, however; all three of these committees were closely linked to traditionally Democratic constituencies. Two other committees that had been proposed for elimination—Veterans' Affairs and Small Business—were ultimately retained despite their limited legislative roles. Unlike the three that were dropped, these committees serve generally Republican constituencies. Table 1 shows the new structure and leadership of the House committee system.

The Republican leadership also diminished the size of most committees and eliminated 25 of the House's 115 subcommittees. Both of these changes were moves to increase the power of committee chairs and, ultimately, of the Speaker who appointed them.

In a more symbolic move, the Republicans renamed a number of committees and made minor changes in committees' jurisdictions. For example, the Education and Labor Committee was renamed Economic and Educational Opportunities to emphasize a new, free-market orientation. Similarly, Government Operations was renamed Government Reform and Oversight to emphasize its focus on improving, rather than merely supervising, the work of the government.

[47]Benjamin Sheffner, "Freshmen Make It to Subcommittee Chairs," *Roll Call*, 15 December 1994

TABLE 1
House Committees, 104th Congress

Committee	Former Name	Chair
Agriculture		Pat Roberts (KS)
Appropriations		Bob Livingston (LA)
Banking and Financial Services	Banking, Finance, and Urban Affairs	Jim Leach (IA)
Budget		John Kasich (OH)
Commerce	Energy and Commerce	Thomas Bliley (VA)
Economic and Educational Opportunities	Education and Labor	Bill Goodling (PA)
Government Reform and Oversight	Government Operations	William Clinger (PA)
House Oversight	House Administration	Bill Thomas (CA)
International Relations	Foreign Affairs	Benjamin Gilman (NY)
Judiciary		Henry Hyde (IL)
National Security	Armed Services	Floyd Spence (SC)
Resources	Natural Resources	Don Young (AK)
Rules		Gerald Solomon (NY)
Science	Science, Space, and Technology	Robert Walker (PA)
Select Intelligence		Larry Combest (TX)
Small Business		Jan Meyers (KS)
Standards of Official Conduct		Nancy Johnson (CT)
Transportation and Infrastructure	Public Works and Transportation	Bud Shuster (PA)
Veterans' Affairs		Bob Stump (AZ)
Ways and Means		Bill Archer (TX)
Committees Eliminated		
	Post Office	
	District of Columbia	
	Merchant Marine and Fisheries	

The only major jurisdictional loser was the former Energy and Commerce Committee, whose portfolio had grown enormously under the forceful and autocratic leadership of John Dingell (D-MI). Under Republican auspices, the committee was shorn of its jurisdiction over railroads, food inspection, inland waterways, the Alaska pipeline, banking regulation, and other areas that Dingell had added to his empire over the years.[48]

[48]Timothy Burger, "Republicans to Cut Size of Most Panels," *Roll Call*, 1 December 1994, p. 1.

Next, the new Republican House leadership eliminated the budgets, staffs, and offices of all House caucuses (formally known as Legislative Service Organizations, or LSOs). Several of the most effective LSOs, including the Black Caucus, the Hispanic Caucus, and the Women's Caucus, were closely tied to the Democratic party. One LSO, the Democratic Study Group, had employed eighteen full-time analysts to help congressional Democrats evaluate proposed and pending legislation. Congress had been spending roughly $4 million per year to support caucus activities. The caucuses will likely continue their activities, however; most announced plans to seek private funding.[49]

Republicans also announced plans to fire hundreds of Democratic committee staffers. Most would not even receive severance pay.[50] At the same time, Republicans planned sharp cuts in the budgets and staffs of the four congressional staff agencies: the General Accounting Office, the Library of Congress, the Congressional Budget Office, and the Office of Technology Assessment. Although these agencies are officially nonpartisan, Republicans believed that they had become too closely identified with the Democrats who had ruled Congress for decades. In all likelihood, once Republicans are satisfied that they have purged the staff agencies of zealous Democratic supporters, they will rebuild them with a more Republican cast. The staff agencies are too useful to Congress to be permanently weakened.

With the support of the Republican leadership and, indeed, much of the Republican House delegation, Gingrich then moved to reduce the influence of committee chairs by limiting them to three consecutive two-year terms; ending the practice of proxy voting, which allowed chairs to control committee votes without the full participation of committee members; and ending the practice of multiple referral, which allowed several committee chairs to claim jurisdiction over one bill. Reducing the power of the committee chairs would almost inevitably enhance the power of the Speaker and the majority leadership, who would now have more control over the appointment of chairs and the referral of bills to committees.

Finally Gingrich moved to change the House rules to make it more difficult to vote tax increases and less difficult to cut spending. Gingrich proposed that a three-fifths vote be required to pass any piece of legislation that included an income tax increase. At the same time, he suggested new procedures that would make it much easier for members to offer so-called limitation amendments to propose cuts in spending bills.

While the House was a beehive of activity, the Senate seemed very quiet as it prepared for the 104th Congress. Senate leaders maintained a strict adherence to the seniority system in the appointment of committee chairs, and made no changes to the committee structure inherited from the Democrats. Gingrich, however, seemed to expand his influence even to the upper chamber with the election of one of his closest allies, Senator Trent Lott of Mississippi, as Senate majority whip. Since the majority leader, Senator Bob Dole of Kansas, is contem-

---

[49]Kenneth Cooper, "GOP Moves to Restrict Office Funds," *Washington Post*, 7 December 1994, p. 1; Alice A. Love, "Already, LSOs Start to Go Private Route," *Roll Call*, 12 December 1994, p. 1.

[50]Gabriel Kahn, "Everyone Gets Fired," *Roll Call*, 5 December 1994, p. 1.

plating a presidential bid, Lott is likely to lead Senate Republicans during much of the session. Lott will no doubt play an important role in promoting Gingrich's priorities in the Senate.

With Newt Gingrich's elevation to the post of Speaker of the House, the shape of the Republican plan is quite clear. As soon as the 104th Congress convened, Gingrich and his allies introduced a package of tax and spending cuts and proposed constitutional amendments based on the Republican "Contract with America" that served as the GOP's platform for the 1994 national elections (see Box 2, page 34).

In an attempt to avoid being marginalized in the legislative process, President Clinton promptly announced his own proposals for cuts in taxes and spending under the rubric of a "middle class bill of rights." Congressional Republicans dismissed the president's proposals as a crass effort to copy the GOP's successful campaign pledges. Even many Democrats felt that the president was in no position to compete with Gingrich and his resurgent congressional Republicans. Democrats hoped that Gingrich would make damaging errors or that conflict would develop between House and Senate Republicans.

Another aspect of the Republicans' strategy is to use legislative investigations to keep the administration off balance and unable to develop its own legislative and policy initiatives. Executive institutions confronted by hostile investigations are typically unable to function effectively. There can be little doubt that the Senate Banking Committee, now chaired by New York Senator Alphonse D'Amato, and its House counterpart, chaired by Iowa Representative Jim Leach, will take long and hard looks at the Whitewater imbroglio.

The results of the 1994 election indicate that President Clinton is likely to have a difficult two years before the next presidential election. Quite possibly, he will face serious challenges for the 1996 Democratic presidential nomination after leading the party to defeat in 1994. It seems certain that his legislative agenda will face strong opposition in Congress.

Republicans, of course, will have their own problems. There is ample potential for friction between Gingrich and the Senate majority leader, Robert Dole, who orchestrated the defeat of Clinton's health care initiative. Republicans, too, may split over their party's 1996 presidential nomination. In the Senate, both Dole and Senator Phil Gramm of Texas are thought to aspire to the presidency. More important, the policies favored by social conservatives, such as restrictions on abortion, are generally opposed by the economic conservatives who form the traditional backbone of the GOP coalition. Members of the latter group often view the social conservatives as a noisy and dangerous rabble who, at best, are a necessary evil if the GOP is to prevail in the electoral arena.

Finally, Republican pledges to cut taxes raise serious fiscal questions. It is by no means clear that these promises can be fulfilled without a serious look at military spending and spending on entitlement programs such as Social Security and Medicare. Yet Republicans have promised to enhance America's military capabilities, and Social Security is defended by political forces even more heavily armed than those that can be mustered by the Pentagon. The shock troops of the American Association of Retired Persons (AARP) stand ready to attack any member of Congress who dares to oppose them.

Nevertheless, the results of the 1994 congressional election offer the Republicans their best chance in a generation to become a long-term majority party. If they are able to implement a program of tax and spending cuts favorable to the interests of middle-class voters, they may complete the work begun by Ronald Reagan and tie the middle-class electorate firmly to the GOP. At the same time, if social and religious conservatives can be satisfied with symbolic victories that do not actually require rank-and-file suburban Republicans to swallow school prayer and restrictions on abortion, the 1994 election may become a major turning point in American political history.

2

Can the Government Govern without Elections?

*T*he obstacles encountered by the Clinton administration bring into sharp focus the problems and dilemmas faced by the United States in the 1990s. What Clinton's difficulties reveal about the process of American government is ultimately far more important than what they tell us about the president. Whatever his own shortcomings, like several of his predecessors, Clinton is the victim of a political process that undermines the U.S. government's capacity to govern.

As we approach the twenty-first century, America faces many problems. Our ability to compete successfully in world markets against other major industrial nations, most notably Japan and Germany, is open to question. America no longer seems able to provide enough jobs or an adequate standard of living for all of its citizens. Our dependence on foreign sources of energy is growing once again. America's position as the world's largest debtor makes the economy and our economic policy increasingly vulnerable to the wishes of foreign bondholders.[1] Our educational system is widely viewed as deserving failing marks. Millions of our fellow citizens lack adequate housing and health care, while our cities are plagued by crime and drugs.

In many instances, programs that are intended to deal with these problems turn out to be more symbol than substance. For example, in 1994, Congress enacted an anti-crime bill in response to the public's growing concern with violence. The bill outlawed the sale of certain types of assault weapons and called for more than $30 billion in federal spending for local anti-crime efforts. These might seem to be important steps in enhancing public safety. Unfortunately, there is some doubt that this legislation will have much impact upon the nation's crime problem. Although 19 types of assault weapons are banned by the bill, 700 types of semiautomatic rifles were exempted from the prohibition, as were any assault weapons already owned at the time the bill was passed. Nearly one-third of the funds promised by the bill were allocated for social "crime prevention" programs such as "midnight sports leagues" and arts activities for inner city neighborhoods—programs that have not been proven to reduce crime. In essence, the 1994 crime bill was an exercise in symbolic politics.[2]

In other areas, such as health care, housing, and education, the U.S. government has seemed unable to formulate or implement effective programs and policies. In still other areas, the government itself is the cause of the nation's problems. For example, the long-term strength of the American economy is threatened by the $4-trillion national debt, the fiscal legacy of the Reagan and Bush presidencies. Despite a general realization that the debt must be brought under control by some combination of tax increases and spending cuts, America's political leadership has thus far been incapable of swallowing the bitter medicine of fiscal discipline.

As we saw earlier, President Clinton did introduce a package of tax increases and spending cuts designed to reduce the federal deficit by hundreds of millions of dollars. And deficit spending did decline somewhat—to roughly $200 billion per year—during the first two Clinton budgets. This was down from $250 billion

---

[1]Douglas R. Sease and Constance Mitchell, "World's Bond Buyers Gain Huge Influence over U.S. Fiscal Plans," *Wall Street Journal*, 6 November 1992, p. 1.

[2]For discussions of the 1994 crime bill, see William Claiborne, "On the Street, Bill's Effectiveness on Crime Reduction Is Debatable," *Washington Post*, 20 August 1994, p. A5; and Ann Devroy, "House Passes $30 Billion Crime Bill," *Washington Post*, 22 August 1994, p. 1.

during the last Bush budget. Indeed, spending caps contained in the 1991 deficit reduction act actually forced the president to reduce spending on domestic programs by nearly $8 billion.[3] The decline in the deficit, however, was not due solely to the president's program; it was just as much a result of low interest rates, which substantially reduced the government's interest obligations on its debt, and of a rise in employment, which produced additional tax revenues. Many experts feared that deficit spending would increase again as soon as interest rates or unemployment began to rise. Projected increases in spending on entitlement programs alone were expected to drive deficit spending back up within the next three to four years.[4] As the nation's economic and social problems have grown, Congress and the White House seem increasingly unable to agree whether to raise taxes, cut spending, raise spending, or cut the deficit. At times, different aspects of federal policy seem to be aimed at each of these objectives simultaneously.

━━━━━━

THE DECLINE OF VOTING AND THE RISE OF "POLITICS BY OTHER MEANS"

An excellent recent volume of essays published by Washington's prestigious Brookings Institution was aptly entitled *Can the Government Govern?* The short answer to this complex question was a very clear "No!"[5] One major reason for our present problems is that over the past several decades an unhealthy and fundamentally undemocratic political process has developed in the United States. The framers of the Constitution believed that a strong government rested most securely upon a broad and active popular base. "I would raise the federal pyramid to a considerable altitude," said Pennsylvania delegate James Wilson. "Therefore, I would give it as broad a base as possible." Concern for the new government's power and stability was a main reason that the framers established representative institutions and permitted political participation on the part of ordinary citizens. For much of U.S. history, the "federal pyramid," indeed, rested upon a relatively broad base of vigorous—often tumultuous—popular participation, with most major issues debated, fought, and ultimately resolved in the electoral arena. America's democratic politics, in turn, provided political leaders with a base of support from which to develop and implement programs, contend with powerful entrenched interests, and during times of crisis, such as the Civil War and World War II, ask the citizenry for the exertions and sacrifices needed in order for the nation to survive. As the framers had intended, democratic politics protected citizens' liberties *and* helped promote governance.

In recent decades, however, popular participation in American political life has declined sharply. Despite a much-ballyhooed increase in voter turnout, only 55.9

[3]David Wessel and David Rogers, "Budget Squeeze," *Wall Street Journal*, 8 February 1994, p. 1.

[4]George Hagar, "The Deficit: Better Than Expected," *Congressional Quarterly Weekly Report*, 25 June 1994, p. 1684.

[5]John Chubb and Paul Petersen, eds., *Can the Government Govern?* (Washington, DC: Brookings Institution, 1989).

percent of eligible Americans bothered to vote in the 1992 presidential election, and barely 39 percent turned out for the 1994 congressional races. At the same time, the political parties that once mobilized voters and imparted a measure of unity to the scattered pieces of the American governmental structure have decayed, making it very difficult, if not impossible, to create a coherent government through the American electoral process.

Both reflecting and reinforcing these changes in the character of elections, the contending political forces in the United States have come to rely heavily on forms of political conflict that neither require nor encourage much in the way of citizen involvement. In recent years, many of the most important national political struggles have been fought largely outside the electoral arena rather than through competitive electoral contests. In fact, in contemporary America, electoral results themselves have at times been negated or reversed by political forces that were not satisfied with the outcomes.

America's contemporary political process—characterized by low voter turnout, weak parties, and the rise of a "politics by other means"—has narrowed the base upon which the "federal pyramid" rests and is the source of many of our government's present problems. As we shall see, this political process is increasingly undemocratic. It fragments political power and fails to provide elected officials with the strong and stable political base they need to govern effectively. Most important, America's contemporary political patterns undermine the ability of elected officials to bring about or even to take account of the public good.

Let's now look critically at the pieces of America's political process with which President Clinton has to work and then consider their implications for his administration's capacity to govern. We will first consider the declining importance of the popular vote and the rise of new forms of political conflict in the United States. Second, we will see how these new forms of conflict undermine governance. Finally, we will attempt to ascertain why there are no easy solutions to America's current political problems. In particular, we will see why, despite their claims to the contrary, major political forces in the United States today are not interested in the one course of action that might restore the government's capacity to govern—the revitalization of the electoral process. This review will help us to understand the problems that afflict Clinton and destroyed five of his six predecessors.

Politics outside the Electoral Arena

For most of U.S. history, elections were the main arenas of political combat. In recent years, however, elections have become less effective as ways of resolving political conflicts in the United States. Today's political struggles are frequently waged elsewhere, with crucial policy choices made outside the electoral realm. Rather than engage voters directly, contending political forces rely on such weapons of institutional combat as congressional investigations, news media revelations, and judicial proceedings. In contemporary America, even electoral success fails to confer the capacity to govern, and political forces, even if they lose at the polls or do not even compete in the electoral arena, have been able to exercise considerable power.

Several trends in contemporary American political life bring sharply into focus the declining significance of the electoral arena. American elections in recent decades have been characterized by strikingly low levels of voter turnout and by a decline of political competition. Since 1900, turnout in national elections has declined by 25 percentage points. In the 1992 presidential election, less than 60 percent of the eligible electorate went to the polls, and in the 1994 midterm congressional elections, voter turnout was a mere 39 percent. In other Western democracies, turnout normally exceeds 80 percent.

The extent to which genuine competition takes place in the electoral arena has also declined sharply in recent decades—especially in congressional races, which tend to be dominated by incumbents who are able to use the resources of their office to turn back any opponents who present themselves. In 1986, 1988, and 1990, 98 percent of the incumbents who sought another term were victorious. Many modern-day congressional races are decided by more than a twenty-point margin, and frequently incumbents face no electoral challenge whatsoever.

In the 1992 general election, despite media claims of an anti-incumbent "mood" in the county, and despite nationwide redistricting, about 95 percent of those incumbents seeking re-election were successful. Even in the electoral earthquake of 1994, more than 91 percent of the incumbents who ran for re-election were successful.

As competition in the electoral arena has declined, the significance of other forms of political combat has risen. Contemporary political struggles have come increasingly to involve the criminal justice system and the courts, the national security apparatus, and the mass media. Let us look at the political role played by each of these non-electoral institutions.

Criminal Indictments   One important substitute for competition in the electoral arena is the growing political use of a powerful non-electoral weapon—the criminal justice system. Since the early 1970s there has been more than a tenfold increase in the number of indictments brought by federal prosecutors against national, state, and local officials. The data given in Figure 2 (page 46) actually understate the extent to which public officials have been subjected to criminal proceedings in recent years, because they do not include those political figures (such as Ronald Reagan's attorney general, Edwin Meese, and former Democratic House Speaker Jim Wright) who were targets of investigations that did not result in indictments.

Many of the individuals indicted have been lower-level civil servants, but large numbers have been prominent political figures—among them more than a dozen members of Congress, several federal judges, and numerous state and local officials. A substantial number of high-ranking Republicans in the executive branch—including former Defense Secretary Caspar Weinberger, former Assistant Secretary of State Elliott Abrams, presidential aides Michael Deaver and Lyn Nofziger, and, of course, national security official Oliver North—were the targets of criminal prosecutions stemming from allegations or investigations initiated by Democrats in Congress. Weinberger and Abrams, along with several other figures in the Iran-Contra case, were pardoned by President George Bush in December 1992, just before he left office. In justifying the pardons, Bush charged that Democrats were attempting to criminalize policy differences.

FIGURE 2

Federal Indictments and Convictions of Public Officials, 1970–1990*

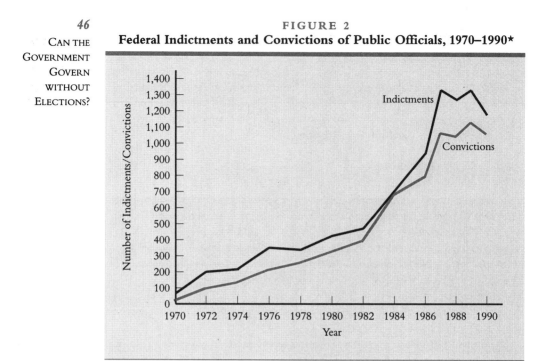

*Reporting procedures were modified in 1983, so pre- and post-1983 data are not strictly comparable.

Source: Annual Reports of the U.S. Department of Justice, Public Integrity Section, 1971–1988; *Statistical Abstract of the United States* (Washington, DC: GPO, 1992), p. 195.

Republicans have also brought allegations of criminal conduct against some of their powerful Democratic opponents. During the first two years of the Clinton administration, the powerful chairman of the House Ways and Means Committee, Dan Rostenkowski, was forced to give up his chairmanship after being indicted on corruption charges; in 1994, he lost what had once seemed to be a permanent seat in the Illinois congressional delegation. That same year, Agriculture Secretary Mike Espy found himself facing allegations that he had illegally accepted trips and other gifts from Tyson Foods, Inc., an Arkansas-based poultry company. Although none of the charges was proven, Espy was forced to resign in October 1994.

There is no particular reason to believe that the level of political corruption or abuse of power in America actually increased tenfold over the past two decades (as Figure 2 would seem to indicate), although it might reflect a heightened level of public concern about governmental misconduct. However, both the issue of government ethics and the growing use of criminal sanctions against public officials have been closely linked to struggles for political power in the United States. In the aftermath of Watergate, institutions such as the office of special counsel were established, and processes for investigating allegations of unethical conduct were created. Since then, political forces have increasingly sought to make use of these mechanisms to discredit their opponents. When scores of investigators, accountants, and lawyers are deployed to scrutinize the conduct of a Jim Wright or a Caspar Weinberger, it is all but certain that something questionable will be

FIGURE 3
Civil Rights Cases Brought in Federal Courts

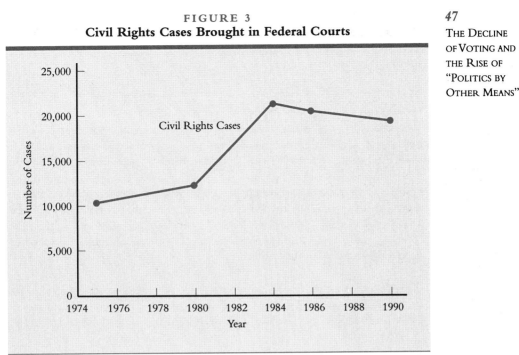

Source: *Statistical Abstract of the United States* (Washington, DC: GPO, 1988, 1989, 1992).

found. So it seems to be the creation of these investigative processes, more than changes in the public's tolerance for government misconduct, that explains the increasing frequency with which public officials are charged with ethical and criminal violations.

The Judiciary   The growing use of criminal indictments as a partisan weapon has further enhanced the political importance of the judiciary. The prominence of the courts has been heightened by the sharp increase in the number of major policy issues that have been fought and decided in the judicial realm rather than in the electoral arena.[6] With the gridlock of politics paralyzing Congress and the president, the federal judiciary has become the main institution for resolving struggles over such issues as race relations and abortion, and has also come to play a more significant role in deciding questions of social welfare and economic policy.[7] The number of suits brought by civil rights, environmental, feminist, and other liberal groups seeking to advance their policy goals increased dramatically during the 1970s and 1980s—reflecting the willingness and ability of these groups to fight their battles in the judicial arena. For example, as Figure 3 indicates, the number of civil rights cases brought in federal courts doubled during this period. After the emergence of a conservative majority on the Supreme Court in 1989, forces on the political right began to use litigation to implement

[6]Jeremy Rabkin, *Judicial Compulsions* (New York: Basic Books, 1989).

[7]Martin Shapiro, "The Supreme Court's 'Return' to Economic Regulation," *Studies in American Political Development* 1 (1986), pp. 91–142.

their own policy agenda. The growing political importance of the federal judiciary explains why Supreme Court confirmation battles, such as the struggle over the Clarence Thomas nomination, came to be so bitterly fought during the Reagan and Bush administrations.[8]

The National Security Apparatus In a similar vein, the national security apparatus has been used extensively as a political weapon in recent decades. During the 1960s and the early 1970s the number of domestic counterintelligence operations directed against groups opposed to the policies of the executive branch expanded substantially. Such activities included wiretaps, surveillance, and efforts to disrupt the activities of the groups.[9] During the 1970s, congressional opposition brought a halt to these counterintelligence efforts; however, recent revelations indicated that in the 1980s, the FBI placed groups opposing the Reagan administration's policies in Central America under surveillance. His administration also relied on the national security apparatus to circumvent and undercut congressional opposition to its policies.

The Media Another institution whose political significance has increased dramatically in recent years is the mass media. With the decline of political parties, politicians have become almost totally dependent upon the media to reach their constituents, and this dependence has made politicians extremely vulnerable to attack by and through the media, whose weapons include, as we saw above, investigative reporting and critical journalism. The national media enhanced their autonomy and political power by aggressively investigating, publicizing, and exposing instances of official misconduct.[10]

Revelation, Investigation, Prosecution

Taken together, the expanded political roles of the national news media and the federal judiciary have given rise to an important new weapon of political combat—revelation, investigation, and prosecution, or RIP, a fitting political epitaph for the public officials who have become its targets. The RIP weaponry was initially forged by opponents of the Nixon administration in their struggles with the White House.

In 1972, after his re-election, President Nixon undertook to expand executive power at the expense of Congress by impounding funds appropriated for domestic programs and reorganizing executive agencies without legislative authorization. In addition, the White House established the so-called plumbers squad of former intelligence agents and mercenaries to plug leaks of information to Congress and the press, and (its opponents claimed) it sought to undermine the legitimacy of the federal judiciary by appointing unqualified justices to the Supreme

---

[8]Martin Shefter, "Institutional Conflict over Presidential Appointments: The Case of Clarence Thomas," *PS: Political Science & Politics* 25, no. 4 (December 1992), pp. 676–78.

[9]William Keller, *The Liberals and J. Edgar Hoover* (Princeton, NJ: Princeton University Press, 1989), Chapter 5.

[10]Samuel P. Huntington, *American Politics: The Promise of Disharmony* (Cambridge: Harvard University Press, 1981), pp. 203–10.

Court. The administration's adversaries also charged that it tried to limit Congress's influence over foreign policy by keeping vital information from it, most notably in the "secret bombing" of Cambodia in 1973.

At the same time, Nixon sought to curtail the influence of the national news media. His administration brought suit against the *New York Times* in an effort to block publication of the Pentagon Papers, a secret, 7,000-page document tracing America's involvement in Vietnam. And, using the pretext of promoting ideological diversity, it threatened to compel the national television networks to sell the local stations they owned. The president's opponents denounced the administration's actions as abuses of power—which they surely were—and launched a full-scale assault upon Richard Nixon over the Watergate controversy.

The Watergate attack began with a series of revelations in the *Washington Post* linking the White House to a break-in at the Democratic National Committee's headquarters at the Watergate Hotel. The *Post's* reporters were quickly joined by scores of investigative journalists from the *New York Times*, *Newsweek*, *Time*, and the television networks.

As revelations of misdeeds by the Nixon White House proliferated, the administration's opponents in Congress demanded a full legislative investigation. In response, the Senate created a special committee, chaired by Senator Sam Ervin, to investigate White House misconduct in the 1972 presidential election. Investigators for the Ervin committee uncovered numerous questionable activities on the part of Nixon's aides, and these were revealed to the public during a series of dramatic, nationally televised hearings.

Evidence of criminal activity unearthed by the Ervin committee led to congressional pressure for the appointment of a special prosecutor. Ultimately, a large number of high-ranking administration officials were indicted, convicted, and imprisoned. Impeachment proceedings were initiated against President Nixon himself, and when evidence was found linking him directly to the cover-up of the Watergate burglary, he was compelled to resign from office. Thus, the RIP weaponry helped the Nixon administration's antagonists achieve total victory in their conflict with the president.

The RIP process became institutionalized when Congress adopted the 1978 Ethics in Government Act, establishing procedures for appointing special prosecutors to deal with allegations of wrongdoing in the executive branch. The act also defined as criminal several forms of influence peddling in which executive officials traditionally engaged, such as lobbying former associates after leaving office. (Such activities are also traditional on Capitol Hill, but Congress chose not to impose the restrictions embodied in the act upon its own members and staff.) Basically, Congress created new crimes with which executive branch officials could be charged.

Opponents of presidential administrations have since used the RIP process to attack and weaken their foes in the executive branch. The extent to which the RIP process has come to be a routine feature of American politics became evident during the Iran-Contra conflict when Democrats charged that the Reagan administration had covertly sold arms to Iran and used the proceeds to provide illegal funding for Nicaraguan Contra forces, in violation of the Boland Amendment, which prohibited such help. After the diversion of funds to the Contras was revealed, it was universally assumed that Congress should conduct televised hearings and the judiciary appoint an independent counsel to investigate the officials involved in the episode. Yet this procedure is really quite remarkable: Officials who would merely be compelled to resign from office in other democracies are here threatened with criminal prosecution.

Republicans were quick to turn the spotlight on the Democrats when Bill Clinton moved into the White House. Congressional Republicans and the conservative news media relentlessly pressed for an investigation of the Clintons' involvement in the Whitewater Development Corporation. The Justice Department finally appointed a special prosecutor, Robert Fiske, to investigate the charges and related accusations that White House aides had made several illegal contacts with Treasury Department officials on behalf of the Clintons. In 1994, Fiske was removed as special counsel and replaced by former federal prosecutor Kenneth Starr. Fiske had been appointed by Attorney General Janet Reno before Congress had restored the lapsed special counsel provision of the Ethics in Government Act. Under the terms of the act, a special counsel is appointed by a panel of federal judges. Once this portion of the act was restored by Congress in 1994, a three-judge federal panel ruled that because Fiske had been appointed to investigate Clinton by a member of Clinton's own cabinet, there was a potential for conflict of interest. Democrats, however, asserted that the Starr appointment represented an even greater conflict of interest; he is a Republican who has been sharply critical of the Clinton administration.[11]

Revelations and investigations of misconduct by public figures have become an important vehicle for political competition in the United States. The primary means through which liberal political forces attacked the White House and mobilized support for themselves during the Reagan administration were the investigations of EPA administrator Anne Burford Gorsuch, Attorney General Edwin Meese, and Supreme Court nominee Robert Bork, as well as the hearings on the Iran-Contra affair.

During the early months of the Bush presidency, partisan warfare chiefly took the form of allegations of misconduct lodged by Democrats and Republicans against one another. Senate Democrats were able to block John Tower's confirmation as secretary of defense with charges that his record of alcohol abuse and sexual impropriety and his ties to defense contractors rendered him unfit to head the Defense Department. Republicans then drove Democratic House Speaker Jim Wright from office with accusations of financial misdeeds, including allegations that Wright and his wife had received large sums of money from a real estate developer and had used inflated royalties from a book contract as a cover for exceeding congressional limits on outside income. At roughly the same time, charges of improper loans and investments compelled Democratic House whip Tony Coelho to resign.

Congressional Democrats responded with allegations that Wright's chief accuser, Republican House whip Newt Gingrich, also reaped improper profits from a book contract and engaged in dubious campaign fund-raising activities. Subse-

---

[11]David Johnston, "Appointment in Whitewater Turns into a Partisan Battle," *New York Times*, 13 August 1994, p. 1.

PROCESS BOX 1

51

THE DECLINE
OF VOTING AND
THE RISE OF
"POLITICS BY
OTHER MEANS"

RIP for Supreme Court Appointments

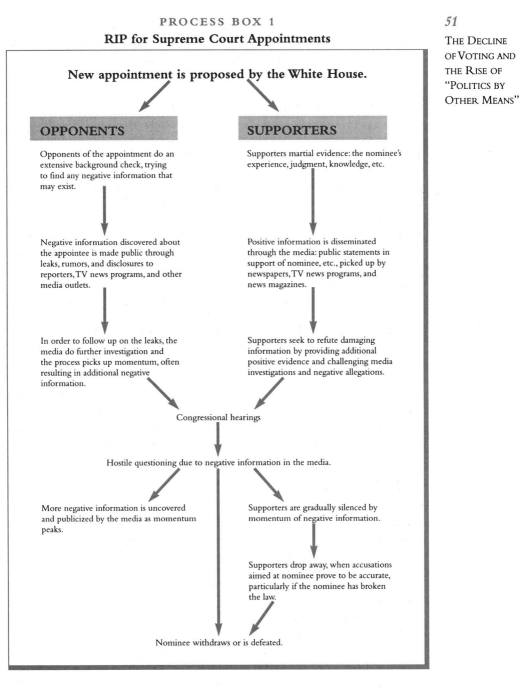

New appointment is proposed by the White House.

OPPONENTS

Opponents of the appointment do an extensive background check, trying to find any negative information that may exist.

Negative information discovered about the appointee is made public through leaks, rumors, and disclosures to reporters, TV news programs, and other media outlets.

In order to follow up on the leaks, the media do further investigation and the process picks up momentum, often resulting in additional negative information.

SUPPORTERS

Supporters martial evidence: the nominee's experience, judgment, knowledge, etc.

Positive information is disseminated through the media: public statements in support of nominee, etc., picked up by newspapers, TV news programs, and news magazines.

Supporters seek to refute damaging information by providing additional positive evidence and challenging media investigations and negative allegations.

Congressional hearings

Hostile questioning due to negative information in the media.

More negative information is uncovered and publicized by the media as momentum peaks.

Supporters are gradually silenced by momentum of negative information.

Supporters drop away, when accusations aimed at nominee prove to be accurate, particularly if the nominee has broken the law.

Nominee withdraws or is defeated.

quently, House Democrats launched an investigation of Republican misuse of funds in the Department of Housing and Urban Development under former secretary Samuel Pierce.

Later, House Republicans called upon Democratic Representative Barney Frank to resign after embarrassing accounts of his personal life appeared in the press. In 1991, Democrats attacked Bush's Supreme Court nominee, Clarence Thomas, with sexual harassment charges, while Republicans assailed the House Democratic leadership with charges that it mismanaged the House bank and post office. In 1992, Democrats called for an investigation of the Bush administration's dealings with Iraq prior to the 1991 Persian Gulf War. They also demanded that a special counsel be appointed to examine allegations that the Bush administration had improperly intervened in a case involving the Atlanta branch of Italy's Banca Nazionale del Lavoro, a bank charged with making illegal loans to Iraq during that nation's war with Iran.[12]

Thus, the RIP process has come to play a central role in national partisan struggles. During the 1980s, politicians, who were elected by popular constituencies, were attacked and driven from office by the opposing party, who used the news media and the courts to accomplish what they couldn't achieve at the polls. This reversal of electoral results "by other means" is profoundly undemocratic, destroys popular confidence in electoral politics, and as we shall see, contributes greatly to the government's inability to govern.

Divided Government, 1968–1992

Non-electoral means of political combat were more widely used during the 1980s and 1990s as a result of two decades of divided government, one party dominating the executive branch, the other the legislative. Since 1968 the Republicans have won all but two presidential elections, while the Democrats have dominated congressional races. As a result, rather than pinning its hopes on defeating its opponent in the electoral arena, each party sought to strengthen the institution it thought that it could be sure of controlling while undermining the one associated with the enemy.

The Republicans reacted to their inability to win control of Congress by seeking to enhance the powers of the White House relative to the legislative branch. As previously mentioned, President Nixon impounded billions of dollars already appropriated by Congress and attempted through various reorganization schemes to bring executive agencies under closer White House control while severing their ties to the House and Senate. Presidents Reagan and Bush tolerated budget deficits of unprecedented magnitude in part because these deficits precluded new congressional spending; they also sought to increase presidential authority over executive agencies and diminish that of Congress by centralizing control over administrative rule making in the the Office of Management and Budget. In addition, Reagan undertook to circumvent the legislative restrictions on presidential conduct embodied in the War Powers Act by sending American military forces abroad without Congressional approval.

The Democrats responded to the Republican presidential advantage by seeking to strengthen Congress while reducing the powers and prerogatives of the presidency—in sharp contrast to their behavior from the 1930s to the 1960s, when the Democratic party enjoyed an advantage in presidential elections. In the

---

[12]George Lardner, Jr., "House Democrats Seek Independent Counsel to Probe Handling of BNL Case," *Washington Post*, 16 October 1992, p. A17.

1970s, Congress greatly enlarged its committee and subcommittee staffs, thus enabling the House and Senate to monitor and supervise closely the activities of executive agencies. Through the 1974 Budget and Impoundment Act, Congress increased its control over fiscal policy. It also enacted a number of statutory restrictions on presidential authority in the realm of foreign policy during the 1970s, including the Foreign Commitments Resolution and the Arms Export Control Act. Finally, congressional investigations, often conducted in conjunction with media exposés and judicial proceedings, were effective in constraining executive power. The most important example is the Iran-Contra affair, which represented the culmination of two decades of struggle over foreign policy.

No More Division?

Bill Clinton's victory in the 1992 presidential election and the following two years of Democratic control of both the White House and Congress did not bring an end to the politics of RIP. Clinton and his supporters represent one faction of the Democratic party and, given America's disjointed and decayed party structure, have little or no capacity to control or discipline other factions. Indeed, during the last Democratic administration, the presidency of Jimmy Carter, liberal Democrats who were dissatisfied with the president's handling of environmental, consumer, and economic policies launched fierce RIP attacks against members of the president's staff.

Thus, it was hardly a surprise when factional conflicts broke out in the Democratic camp immediately after the 1992 election.[13] Nor was it surprising that, even before Clinton's inauguration, the president-elect's cabinet appointees came under RIP attack. Clinton's commerce secretary-designate Ron Brown, assailed for vigorously soliciting corporate and interest group contributions for an inaugural affair in his honor, quickly canceled the event and was able to weather the storm because the host of Democratic politicians for whom he had raised funds over the years rallied to his defense.[14]

At the same time, Zoë Baird, Clinton's choice for attorney general, was attacked for employing as household workers a Peruvian couple who had entered the United States illegally and for not securing appropriate documentation or making Social Security payments for them. Baird made a large payment retroactively and paid a fine. Nevertheless, after two days of hostile questioning by members of the Senate Judiciary Committee and a deluge of letters and phone calls to members of Congress from individuals and groups protesting the nomination, Baird asked the president to withdraw her name. Clinton, eager to contain the damage from what came to be called "nannygate," hardly bothered to defend his nominee and quickly rescinded the appointment.[15]

[13]See Thomas B. Edsall, "Cracks in the Clinton Coalition," *Washington Post*, 8 November 1992, p. C1. See also Elizabeth Drew, "The White House's New New Dealers," *Washington Post*, 8 November 1992, p. C1.

[14]Paul Barrett and David Rogers, "Senate Support for Zoë Baird is Precarious," *Wall Street Journal*, 22 January 1993, p. A3.

[15]Ruth Marcus and David Broder, "President Takes Blame for Rushing Baird Selection," *Washington Post*, 23 January 1993, p. A1.

The campaign against Baird, according to some observers, was organized and orchestrated not by Republicans but by Democratic liberals. Consumer advocate Ralph Nader and other liberals objected to Baird's background as a corporate lawyer and to her past support for tort law reforms that would restrict citizen suits.[16] Some Republicans cheerfully joined the attack, happy to have an opportunity to give Clinton a black eye during his first week in office. Curiously, though, Baird's chief defender during the Senate confirmation process was conservative Republican Senator Orrin Hatch of Utah, who was delighted that Clinton had nominated someone without close ties to liberal advocacy groups for the position of attorney general.

Several months later, conservative forces used the RIP weapon against the liberals. The Lani Guinier nomination, discussed earlier, was scuttled when conservative activists led by Clint Bolick of the Institute for Justice, a libertarian think tank, began to send excerpts from Guinier's scholarly writings to journalists, congressional staffers, and other opinion makers. Bolick and his associates also wrote press releases, reports, and op-ed pieces characterizing Guinier as an extremist. Bolick acknowledged that he was seeking to make use of the same techniques used so successfully by liberal forces over the preceding years. "There's no question," he said, "that in terms of tactics, the playbook was written by the left and we're playing by the rules of the game established over the last 12 years."[17]

Several other of Clinton's appointees were targeted with the RIP process and forced out of their positions during the first two years of the Democratic administration. Most notably, Deputy Treasury Secretary Robert Altman was accused of allowing improper contacts between Treasury Department officials and White House staff members during the initial stages of the Whitewater investigation, and of failing to remove himself from the case at the outset despite a clear conflict of interest. After weeks of criticism and arduous testimony before Congress, Altman resigned. Later that year, in an unrelated case, Agriculture Secretary Mike Espy was also forced to resign following charges of ethics violations.

These rumblings of RIP artillery show that the end of the era of divided government did not bring about the end of politics by other means. In the Baird case, liberal Democratic forces that had been defeated by more moderate Democrats in the presidential electoral arena did not hesitate to attack their factional rivals with the same weaponry they had previously used against the Republicans. In the Guinier case it was conservative activists wielding the artillery. Now that divided government has returned to Washington, RIP no doubt will continue to be a weapon of partisan and factional struggle in the years to come. Indeed, even before the 1994 elections, House Republican whip Newt Gingrich promised that, if Republicans won control of the Congress, they would hold extensive hearings on matters such as the Whitewater affair. With Republicans firmly in control of both houses, it is certain that Whitewater will be thoroughly investigated by House and Senate committees.

[16]Michael Isikoff and Ruth Marcus, "As Support for Baird Erodes, Senators Call for Withdrawal," *Washington Post*, 22 January 1993, p. 1. See also Seymour Martin Lipset, "Roosevelt Redux for the Democrats," *Wall Street Journal*, 21 January 1993, p. A14.

[17]Michael Isikoff, "Power Behind the Thrown Nominee: Activist with Score to Settle," *Washington Post*, 6 June 1993, p. A11.

In the meantime, of course, Democrats were quick to charge House Speaker Gingrich with ethical violations of his own. Gingrich had signed a lucrative multi-million-dollar book contract with Harper/Collins Publishers, a corporation controlled by publishing magnate Rupert Murdoch. Democrats charged that Gingrich was seeking to "cash in" on his position, and some even hinted that the entire book deal might be an effort by Murdoch to enlist the Speaker's help in dealing with the various regulatory and licensing problems facing his far-flung communications empire.[18]

55

CAN
DEMOCRATIC
POLITICS
FUNCTION
WITHOUT
VOTERS?

And so, RIP continues. Let us consider now the implications this will have for democratic politics and governance.

CAN DEMOCRATIC POLITICS FUNCTION WITHOUT VOTERS?

During the political struggles of the past decades, politicians sought to undermine the institution associated with their foes, disgrace one another on national television, force their competitors to resign from office, and in a number of cases, send their opponents to prison. Remarkably, one tactic that has not been so widely used is the mobilization of the electorate. Of course, Democrats and Republicans continue to contest each other in national elections. Voter turnout even inched up in 1992. But neither side has made much effort to mobilize new voters, to create strong local party organizations, or in general, to make full use of the electoral arena to defeat its enemies.

It is certainly not true that politicians don't know how to mobilize new voters and expand electoral competition. In fact, if politicians have a strong enough incentive, they demonstrate that they do know how to mobilize voters. For example, a massive get-out-the-vote effort by Democrats to defeat neo-Nazi David Duke in the 1991 Louisiana Democratic gubernatorial primary led to a voter turnout of over 80 percent of those eligible—twice the normal turnout level for a Louisiana primary. How extraordinary, then, that politicians who will stop at nothing in their efforts to RIP the opposition stop short of attempting to expand the electorate to overwhelm their foes in competitive elections. Why is this?

Party organization is an especially important instrument for enhancing the political influence of groups at the bottom of the social hierarchy—groups whose major political resource is numbers. Parties allow politicians to organize the energies of large numbers of individuals from the lower classes to counter the superior financial and institutional resources available to those from the middle and upper classes. But political party organizations have declined over the past several decades.

This decline, resulting in large measure from the efforts of upper- and middle-class "reformers," over the years, has undermined politicians such as union officials and Democratic and Republican "machine" leaders who had a stake in

[18]David Streitfield, "$4 Million Book Deal for Gingrich: Political Foes Decry Windfall from Murdoch Firm," *Washington Post*, 22 December 1994, p. 1.

Do Elections and Voting Matter?

*M*ost Americans take pride in the country's annual election rituals, pointing out that few nations of the world have mechanisms for transferring power in such a smooth and peaceful fashion. Critics of American elections argue, however, that the differences between the candidates and political parties are marginal, if not non-existent; that elections and campaigns are more spectacle than shows of real power; and that elections pacify the electorate more than they encourage true citizenship.

Political scientists Gerald M. Pomper and Susan S. Lederman argue that elections in fact do meet the criteria for meaningful political exercises. Political scientist Howard L. Reiter, on the other hand, argues that voting is at best a poor method for translating preferences into policies and, worse, that voting tends to channel citizens toward a relatively harmless political act and away from other, more effective methods of political expression.

Pomper and Lederman

The first necessity for meaningful elections is an organized party system. . . . Without a choice between at least two competing parties, the electorate is powerless to exert its influence.

A related vital requirement is for free competition between the parties. The voters must be able to hear diverse opinions and be able to make an uncoerced choice. . . . Nomination and campaigning must be available to the full range of candidates, and the means provided for transmitting their appeals to the electorate. . . .

Elections in the United States do largely meet the standards of meaningful popular decisions; true voter influence exists. The two parties compete freely with one another, and the extent of their competition is spreading to virtually all states. Access to the voters is open to diverse candidates, and no party or administration can control the means of communication. Suffrage is virtually universal, and voters have fairly simple choices to make for regular offices. In the overwhelming number of cases, voting is conducted honestly. . . .

Whatever the future may hold, present conditions in the United States do enable the voters to influence, but not control, the government. The evidence . . . does not confirm the most extravagant expectations of popular sovereignty. Neither are elections demonstrably dangerous or meaningless. Most basically, we have found the ballot to be an effective means for the protection of citizen interests. Elections in America ultimately provide only one, but the most vital, mandate.[1]

Reiter

Most of the major issues in American history have been resolved not by elections but by other historical forces. . . . Elections are not very good ways of expressing the policy views of the people who actually vote. Elections are even less effective as a means of carrying out the policy views of all citizens. . . .

Politics, we are encouraged to believe, occurs once a year in November, and for most adults it occurs only once every four years. We are able to discharge our highest civic function by taking a few minutes to go into a booth and flip a few levers once every four years. Although we are all free to engage in other political activities, such as collective action, writing to officials or working on campaigns, most adults are quite content to limit their political activity to that once-in-a-quadrennium lever flip. And if we think of voting as the crown jewel of our liberties, we will not think that citizenship requires anything else.

All in all, the message that elections sends us is to be passive about politics. Don't take action that involves any effort, don't unite with other citizens to achieve political goals, just respond to the choice that the ballot box gives us. In a strange way, then, elections condition us *away* from politics. A nation which defines its precious heritage in terms of political right discourages its citizens from all but the *least* social, *least* public, and *least* political form of activity. This should raise the most profound questions for us. Why should we as a society discourage political activism? What is the real role that voting plays in our politics?[2]

[1]Gerald M. Pomper and Susan S. Lederman, *Elections in America: Control and Influence in Democratic Politics*, 2nd ed. (New York: Longman, 1980), pp. 223–25.

[2]Howard L. Reiter, *Parties and Elections in Corporate America* (New York: St. Martin's Press, 1987), pp. 1–3, 9.

popular mobilization, while it strengthened politicians with an upper-middle- or upper-class base. As a result, today's Democratic and Republican parties are dominated by different segments of the American upper-middle class. For the most part, contemporary Republicans speak for business interests and professionals from the private sector, while Democratic politicians and political activists are drawn from and speak for upper-middle-class professionals in the public and not-for-profit sector.

Both sides pay lip service to the idea of fuller popular participation in political life. But since politicians and their upper-middle-class constituents in both camps have access to a variety of different political resources—the news media, the courts, universities, and interest groups, to say nothing of substantial financial resources—neither side has much need for or interest in political tactics that might, in effect, stir up trouble from below. Both sides prefer to compete for power without engaging in full-scale popular mobilization. What we are left with, then, is a political process whose class bias is so obvious and egregious that, if it continues, Americans may have to begin adding a qualifier when describing politics as democratic, using terms like "semi-democratic," "quasi-democratic," or "neo-democratic" to describe a political process in which ordinary voters have as little influence as they do in contemporary America.

POLITICS AND GOVERNANCE

Party politicians of old had stable, organized, popular followings that could be counted upon when their leaders came under fire. As Chicago's longtime machine mayor, Richard J. Daley, once said in response to media attacks, "When you've got the people behind you, you don't need the media. . . . The media can kiss my ———!" Contemporary politicians seldom have well-organized popular followings. Lacking such a base of support, they seldom can afford Mayor Daley's indifference to his media image. This failure to organize and mobilize a strong popular base leaves today's politicians weak and vulnerable to the institutions and interests, including the mass media, upon which they are now so dependent. As we saw, President Clinton is no exception; he could not afford to reach over, never mind behind, the news media.

This lack of popular support in contemporary American politics undermines governance in four ways. First, it means that elections today fail to accomplish what must be the primary task of any leadership selection process: They fail to award the winners with the power to govern. Under the fragmented system bequeathed to us by the Constitution's framers, seldom have all the levers of power been grasped by a unified and disciplined party or group. Today, however, with the decay of America's political party organizations, this fragmentation has increased sharply. There are many victorious cliques and factions with little unity among them. During the Bush presidency, fragmentation and division led to a pattern of "gridlock" in which little or nothing could be accomplished in Washington; this paralysis resurfaced after the first few months of the Clinton presidency, and struck with a vengeance during the second year of his term.

Second, since elected officials lack a firm base of popular support, they are particularly vulnerable to RIP attacks. Often they find that their standing in public opinion polls (today's substitute for an organized popular base) has evaporated overnight, their capacity to govern disappearing with it. Thus, the Nixon administration was paralyzed for three years by the Watergate affair and the Reagan White House for two years by Iran-Contra. Congress was nearly immobilized for a year by the Tower-Wright-Coelho-Frank imbroglio and for another year by the House bank and post office scandal. During his first six months in office, Clinton, too, was distracted by the Baird and Guinier fiascoes. This is hardly a recipe for a government able to solve America's long-term deficit and trade problems.

Third, because they lack a strong popular base, politicians seldom have the capacity to confront entrenched economic or political interest groups, even when the public interest seems clear. For example, early in the Bush administration, the Treasury Department planned to resolve the crisis in the savings and loan (S&L) industry by imposing a fee on S&L deposits. But this idea was adamantly rejected by the industry and met overwhelming resistance on Capitol Hill, where thrift institutions enjoyed a good deal of influence. So the administration was compelled to disown the Treasury plan and proposed, instead, a plan in which general tax revenues would finance the bulk of the $166 billion bailout. In this way, a powerful interest, the S&L industry, was able to shift the burden of a major federal initiative designed for the industry's own benefit from itself to the general public. Moreover, to mask the impact of the bailout on the nation's budget deficit, it was largely financed through "off-budget" procedures—a ploy that disguises the costs initially but over time adds billions of dollars to the bailout tab.

In a similar vein, after his election in 1992, President Clinton felt compelled to reassure the nation's business community and powerful banking and financial interests that his administration would be receptive to their needs. So even though he campaigned as a staunch opponent of business-as-usual in Washington, he named Democratic National Committee Chair Ron Brown to be his secretary of commerce and Texas Democratic Senator Lloyd Bentsen to the post of secretary of the treasury. Brown was a veteran Washington corporate lobbyist well known to the business community. Bentsen, as chair of the Senate Finance Committee, was noted for his close and cordial relationship with banking, finance, insurance, and real estate interests.[19] President Clinton was no more eager than his predecessor to confront these Goliaths.

Later, to secure the enactment of his tax proposals, Clinton felt compelled to give major tax concessions to a variety of interests including aluminum producers, real estate developers, multinational corporations, and segments of the energy industry.[20] Other interest groups quickly decided that the president had little capacity to resist their demands. In March 1993 several Western senators speaking for grazing, timber-cutting, and mining groups, alarmed by a Clinton proposal to increase fees for the use of federal lands, visited the president and were able to extract quick concessions. "The message was unmistakable," said one lobbyist. "If you can exert enough influence on your members of Congress and get them to transmit the pressure to the administration, you have a strong chance of not having to share as much sacrifice as some other folks.[21] Before he dropped his proposal for a "Btu Tax," Clinton had already given in to so many demands for exemptions by industry groups that projected revenues from the tax had already fallen by a third. One Washington lobbyist reported that the Clinton administration was asking so little in return for tax breaks that his client was able to secure a requested tax change even without agreeing to endorse the proposed tax in return.[22] Subsequently, Clinton was compelled to abandon the Btu tax altogether, when he could not overcome opposition led by Senator David Boren, a member of the Senate Finance Committee and a strong supporter of the energy industry.

Similarly, President Clinton made so many concessions to powerful interest groups on the health care plan he unveiled in September 1993 that the entire program's fiscal viability was seriously jeopardized. Because senior citizens opposed a loss of current benefits, Medicare recipients were not only exempted from the plan; they were also promised expensive new benefits under the Medicare system. Because the politically powerful postal workers' union was determined to continue administering its own generous health-insurance program,

---

[19]Jill Abramson and John Harwood, "Some Say Likely Choice of Bentsen, the Insider, for Treasury Post Could Send the Wrong Signals," *Wall Street Journal*, 9 December 1992, p. A26.

[20]David Hilzenrath, "Bentsen Signals White House's Willingness to Deal," *Washington Post*, 17 May 1993, p. A4.

[21]David Broder and Michael Weisskopf, "Return to Gridlock," *Washington Post*, 13 June 1993, p. 1.

[22]Timothy Noah, "BTU Tax is Dying Death of a Thousand Cuts as Lobbyists Seem to Be Able to Write Own Exemptions," *Wall Street Journal*, 8 June 1993, p. A18.

it also demanded and received exemption from the Clinton plan. Other public employee unions vowed to seek similar treatment for their own members. As a concession to veterans' groups, the Veterans Administration's medical system was exempted from the plan as well. Following suit, physicians' groups demanded and won the incorporation of provisions that would allow them to continue to practice fee-for-service medicine, and large corporations were permitted to opt out of the plan despite the fact that their health care costs would decline as the federal government began to pick up the tab for citizens who previously had no health insurance. All these concessions were made *before* the plan was even introduced.[23] Once the plan was actually submitted to Congress, other powerful interests demanded and received costly special considerations. Like the Btu tax, the 1994 efforts to reform health care died the death of a thousand concessions as the need to purchase the support of powerful interests simply overwhelmed fiscal realities.

Finally, the enhanced political power of non–electoral institutions, unchecked by a robust electorate, means that the question of who will not govern is unlikely to be resolved in the voting booth. Electoral defeat today does not deprive the losing party of the power to undermine the programs and policies of the winner. Indeed, as we have seen, electoral verdicts can now be reversed outside the electoral arena. So "winners" and "losers" typically engage in a continuing struggle, which often distracts them from real national problems. For example, in 1991 and 1992, official Washington seemed much more concerned with several thousand dollars in bounced congressional checks than with several hundred billion dollars in debts.

More important, however, this struggle compels politicians to pay greater heed to the implications of policies for their domestic political battles than for collective national purposes. A major reason the Reagan and Bush administrations were prepared to accept the economic risks of unprecedented deficits is the constraint these deficits imposed on congressional power. Similarly, the Republicans pressed for deregulation in part because the constellations of interests surrounding many regulatory policies are important Democratic bastions. This sort of political gamesmanship caused the administration to overlook the potential costs and risks of their policies. For instance, the relaxation of regulatory restraints on financial institutions permitted many S&Ls to shift from their traditional role as home mortgage lenders into potentially more lucrative but dangerously speculative areas. We now all know the results.

Concern for their own institutional and political advantage can also affect the way officials respond to the initiatives of their opponents. For example, congressional Democrats regularly voted for lower levels of military spending than the two Republican administrations proposed, not because they were less committed to the nation's defense, but because the defense establishment has been an institutional stronghold of the Republicans. This fact also played a part in Democratic opposition to the 1991 Persian Gulf War. Similarly, despite the continuing problem of America's huge budget deficit, the Clinton administration has been committed

---

[23]See Steven Pearlstein and Dana Priest, "Ensuring a Healthy Chance: Reform Plan Tailored to Attract Base of Allies," *Washington Post*, 22 September 1993, p. 1. See also, Jeffrey Birnbaum, "Clinton Health Package Has a Little Something for Just Enough Factions to Splinter Opposition," *Wall Street Journal*, 23 September 1993, p. A18.

to increases in federal domestic spending. Like Reagan's and Bush's reasons for keeping defense spending high, domestic social spending is politically necessary for the Clinton administration, whatever the long-term economic risks it may entail. Indeed, despite his reputation as a "policy wonk," Clinton quickly found that it was virtually impossible to focus on questions of policy effectiveness. Purely political considerations frequently had to come first.[24] In contemporary America, political struggle is constant, leaving little room for consideration of the greater public good.

---

[24]See Jeffrey H. Birnbaum and Michael K. Frisby, "Clinton's Zigzags between Politics and Policy Explain Some Problems of His First 100 Days," *Wall Street Journal*, 29 April 1993, p. A16.

3

The State of American Politics Today and Tomorrow

November 8, 1994, was a disaster for the Democrats in general and for President Clinton in particular. The Republicans gained control of the entire Congress—House as well as Senate—in the biggest and sweetest Republican victory since 1946. Republicans also came out of the 1994 election with a gain of 10 governorships, from 20 to 30, and control of 17 state legislatures, up from 8. These changes will have tremendous bearing on the 1996 presidential election, and the Democrats are first to recognize it. As the *Washington Post* essayist Meg Greenfield put it, "Something indisputably dire has been said by the voters to the Democrats. The problem lies in the difficulty they are having deciding what it was that was said and what they should do about it."[1]

But those same Democrats should also be asking why. From a purely political standpoint, Bill Clinton had done almost everything right. As a candidate, he had overcome enormous odds, justifiably earning the title, "The Comeback Kid." As a candidate and as president, Clinton had brought the Democratic party more and more into what had been defined as the Center or Mainstream—that is, he had brought the Democratic party closer and closer to the Republican party, the party of Ronald Reagan. That had in fact been the objective of the Democratic Leadership Council (DLC), of which Bill Clinton had been a founder. Is it right that things should go so wrong for such a responsible political party and so accommodating a political leader?

How wrong did things go? Most knowledgeable observers with any sense of history at all tend to minimize the significance of midterm elections. In the first place, the party of every first-term president loses seats in the House and Senate in the first congressional election following the presidential victory. Second, since the midterm is not one national election but 435 House elections and at least 33 Senate elections, a single, national interpretation is rarely if ever sustainable. Third, despite the stridency and intensity of certain Republican leaders, and despite the Contract with America they so prominently display, few of the 435 House and 35 Senate contests were fought over national issues. Moreover, four out of ten voters said in the exit polls that their voting for the House candidate of their choice had nothing to do with Bill Clinton.[2] Another indication of the character of voting in 1994 can be found in that infamous incumbency re-election rate. Since 1954, the rate of incumbent re-election to the House of Representatives has fallen below 90 percent only twice, in 1964 and 1974 (88.4 and 89.6 percent, respectively). Between 1968 and 1992, the *average* incumbency re-election rate was 95.2 percent. In 1994, the incumbent re-election rate fell to 91.1 percent, compared to 96.3 percent in 1990, President Bush's midterm congressional election. But here's the rub for the Democrats: Virtually all incumbents defeated in 1994 were Democrats. Whatever problems this may give President Clinton in the next two years of his term, the fact remains that the vote was against incumbents and *the government*, and not against the policies or the person of President Clinton. There is an old saying among junior members of Congress: "When in doubt, vote 'No.'" The same principle is often observed by the American electorate: "When in

---

[1]Meg Greenfield, "Strategists without a Clue," *Newsweek*, 5 December 1994, p. 90.

[2]Exit polls from Richard Berke, "Victories Were Captured by GOP Candidates, Not for the Party's Platform," *New York Times*, 10 November 1994, p. B1.

doubt about the government, or when you feel your opinions are having no influence, vote 'No.'"

So, what was the nature of the disaster that befell the Democratic party and the Democratic president and the Democratic agenda in 1994? To explain that is to shed some new light on the presidency and the whole national political establishment. Our concern is not with President Clinton or his personal plight. That is for his advisers and his party. Our concern is for the state of our national institutions of government and their capacity to govern.

Our assessment has three dimensions. The first dimension is the national power structure—the prevailing political coalitions and the beliefs and values that validate these coalitions and provide them their lasting popular constituencies. The second dimension is Bill Clinton and the New Democrats—how they fit and why they don't. The third dimension is the contemporary American political process itself—in particular, the diminished political possibilities available in American democracy and the peril it faces as a consequence.

THE NEW NATIONAL POWER STRUCTURE

Although we have a Democrat in the White House, the coalition that made Democratic presidents particularly strong as well as activist is no longer in place. In Chapter 1 we discussed the causes of the collapse of the New Deal coalition, which was led by Southern white politicians and Northern urban machine bosses and labor leaders. In the 1960s, liberal activists attacked and destroyed the power of the machine bosses and labor leaders. In addition, the Civil Rights movement curtailed the power of Southern white politicians by enfranchising millions of African American voters in the South. As a result, the New Deal coalition collapsed, and the Democratic party was dramatically changed. As we saw in Chapter 2, the aftermath of this change has had serious consequences for the presidency and the state of American politics. Now let's assess more closely the new national power structure that has arisen since the early 1970s and how this power structure shapes the nation's governance.

The Liberal Tradition in America

Over the last two decades, Republicans have attempted to taint Democrats with charges of being excessively liberal. When Newt Gingrich called Bill Clinton a "McGovernick" or claimed Clinton was showing "his true liberal colors," he was repeating a fashion started by Ronald Reagan to label Democrats as left-wingers. Reagan charged that any programs the Democrats favored that put any restraint on the free market were radically Leftist, "out of the mainstream," and even un-American. But what is the Left?

Reagan was correct about one thing: Something cannot be truly Left unless it is deliberately anti-capitalism. That is the essential definition of the Left as understood historically in Europe, from whence the term came. The Left—meaning socialism—sees capitalism as a moral problem. American liberals, on the other hand, including the liberals in the mainstream of the Democratic party, see capitalism as good because it works, although it is imperfect and occasionally needs a boost or a restraint. This kind of pragmatic pro-capitalism is the quintessence of liberalism.

Thus, when you consider the true meaning of the label "Left," it is clear that the charges aimed at Clinton were inherently inaccurate. His policies were much closer to the Republicans' ideal than they were to the Socialists'. This brings us to two truths relevant to the contemporary policy dialogue in Washington. Truth One: There is virtually no Left left in America, and what there is of it is not in the Democratic party. Truth Two: The mainstream of the Republican party is *not* conservative, but liberal, and it always has been liberal. It has a conservative wing, and that wing is growing larger and more influential, as we shall see, but the party, as a whole, is not conservative.

To keep matters consistent as well as accurate, we have referred to the Republican party as "Old liberal," not because it is old-fashioned, but because it came first. It is the party of Adam Smith, the party first to embrace capitalism and markets as so promising that they deserved protection and nourishing, by government where necessary. The Democratic party, being mainly a Southern party in the nineteenth century, is the party of "New liberalism" in the twentieth century, because it replaced a discredited GOP in 1932 and appropriated the liberal label at the same time.

Thus the difference between the two major parties is a difference of degree. This difference of degree is meaningful because it differentiates the two traditional constituencies of the parties—one tending toward the lower income and social scales with a preference for trying to reduce risk in society through public policies, and the other constituency on the upper income and social scales with a preference for letting risk reach its own level. More government versus less government is part of the difference between New and Old liberalism, but make no mistake about it: Both parties are liberal parties, with the Republicans being, by degree, harder to convince that a particular imperfection in capitalism can be improved upon deliberately as a matter of policy. This is not to say that Old liberals (Republicans) are anarchists. Some kinds of government are acceptable to them—policing, contract enforcement, or protecting the integrity of the professions of law, medicine, and accounting, for example. National defense is nothing but a bundle of government policies. It's all a matter of degree.

The Conservative Tradition in America

Conservatism, or as they would say in Europe, the Right, is not merely the far end of a simple continuum with New liberal on the left and Old liberal in the center. As the inimitable Meg Greenfield put it, "We should get rid of this intellectually tyrannizing, thought-deforming concept of the 'spectrum' altogether, the supposedly reliable depiction of which positions can be said to lie at precisely which point from the Left to 'moderate' Center to Right along an imaginary band."[3] But Greenfield does not go far enough. The genuine conservatives are essentially the

---

[3]Greenfield, "Strategists without a Clue."

FIGURE 4

67

THE NEW
NATIONAL
POWER
STRUCTURE

Traditions of American Political Thought

Epochs	Positions	
	Liberal	*Conservative*
Old	**1** *Old Liberalism* *Tenets:* Individual above all, the pursuit of happiness, free market, capitalism *Justification for government:* Intervention only against conduct that is palpably harmful *in its consequences* *Ideal:* A society free *for* risk *Examples (& people):* Mainstream Republican party, libertarians (Adam Smith, Milton Friedman, Jack Kemp) *Would support:* Privatization, deregulation, end of welfare state, abortion rights	**3** *Old Conservatism* *Tenets:* Morality above all, the individual is subordinate to morality, in society and politics *Justification for government:* Intervention against conduct deemed good or evil *in itself* *Ideal:* A *good* society, by sacred standards *Examples (& people):* Secular Right (William Buckley, George Will, William Bennett, Newt Gingrich), Christian Right (Pat Robertson, Ralph Reed, Dan Quayle) *Would support:* School prayer, morally strict welfare state, right to life
New	**2** *New Liberalism* *Tenets:* Same as Box 1, but more statist *Justification for government:* Same as Box 1, but with a lower threshold: the *theory* of harm is enough *Ideal:* A society free *from* risk *Examples (& people):* Traditional Democratic party, unions (Mario Cuomo, Jay Rockefeller, Richard Gephardt) *Would support:* Broad health coverage, minimum wage, gun control, abortion rights	**4** *New Conservatism* *Tenets:* Same as Box 3 *Justification for government:* Same as Box 3 *Ideal:* A virtuous society *Examples (& people):* Neo-conservatives, Heritage Foundation, converts from Left and liberal groups (Irving Kristol, Thomas Sowell, Jeane Kirkpatrick) *Would support:* Interventionist foreign policy, morality through antiquity, anti-affirmative action

moralists among us. That puts them off the spectrum that liberals occupy. Although they are, as they profess to be, pro-capitalism, they are nevertheless uncomfortable with the pure acquisitiveness of the free market—recalling that acquisitiveness is a synonym for greed. The Declaration of Independence, being a liberal document, espouses "the pursuit of happiness," which is as liberal as one can get. The pragmatism, positivism, and scientism of the liberal is also bothersome to the genuine conservative. Morality should come first—it is the transcendent value.

The conservative tradition in America comes in two parts: the religious Right and the secular Right. Both see markets and government as subordinate to a transcendent moral code, based on traditional sources. For the religious Right, these sources come from the Scripture; for the secular Right, the sources come from tradition and community. For conservatives, these sources must serve as the basis not only of personal behavior, but of public policy as well.

Figure 4 attempts to capture logically those ideologies. Each of the four boxes within the figure contains the ideas and values that we call ideology. These boxes also give examples of groups and individuals who are visible proponents of these ideologies, as well as examples of current policy issues that each group might tend to support. Putting the policies in separate boxes indicates pictorially that policies don't belong on a single spectrum. The passage from one to another is not smooth but involves abrupt turnings of corners and crossings of ideological borders. Moreover, people and groups tend to straddle the borders from one ideology to another; almost all liberals are conservative some of the time on some things, and most genuine conservatives are liberals or make common cause with liberals some of the time on some issues. Ideologies are broadly constructed tendencies based on our values. They guide our preferences, making it easier for us to choose between important alternatives without having always to go back to square one. And, as we shall see, people shift in the emphases they put on their conservative selves and their liberal selves. This is why we have epochs and cycles in which one ideology declines and another rises.

Likewise, political parties do not always fall into one or another ideological box. For instance, the New Deal coalition in the Democratic party was a coalition of boxes 2 and 3 (the traditional "New liberal" Democrats and the Southern conservatives, respectively). Its "collapse" was due largely to the alienation of the Southern conservative wing of the party.[4]

For much of America's political history, the Right has appeared almost invisible. For instance, the Southern conservatives who formed part of the Democrats' New Deal coalition were willing to play second fiddle to the Northern Roosevelt liberals because the conservatives were genuinely troubled about the evils of capitalism. Conservatives' concern for family values, community, tradition, and home ownership led directly to the fear of the power of money, the pursuit of wealth for its own sake, absentee ownership, and impersonal corporate ownership. Even today, hardly a day passes without an attack on business, the media, or other members of the Eastern establishment by Southern conservatives.[5] As long as the New Deal Democratic party stayed away from race, as it did until the 1960s, a strong, liberal New Deal was acceptable to the Southern conservatives. Their counterparts in the Republican right wing, far smaller in number and influence, also seemed content to accept the crumbs of second-class citizenship within the Republican party.

But this apparent passivity of the Right and its members' lack of national visibility does not mean they were any less political. Conservatives did not call attention to themselves in the national media because most of the political issues of concern to them were state and local issues. For example, on such matters as family laws, divorce laws, morality laws, abortion and adoption laws, education laws, or election laws, going to Washington would have been a waste of time. Most action on these

[4]Southern Democrats had tried twice before to split off completely from the New Deal Democratic party. In 1948, Southern Democrats formed the Dixiecrat party; in 1968, George Wallace tried it again with his American Independent party.

[5]For an instructive assessment of the anti-establishment views of Jesse Helms, see John Podhoretz, "Helms: A Contrarian Who Never Forgets, or Forgives," *Los Angeles Times*, 4 December 1994, p. M1. For the views of another important Southern conservative on the evils of high finance, bankers, and the Eastern establishment, see Pat Robertson, *The New World Order* (Dallas: Word, 1991), pp. 122ff. For a good discussion of Robertson's views on the "manipulative power of large financial institutions," and his denunciation of "the money trust, monopoly bankers, money barons, the capitalist cartel and the 'establishment,'" see Allen D. Hertzke, *Echoes of Discontent* (Washington: CQ Press, 1993), pp. 85–92.

matters even today, and even more so prior to the New Deal, occurred in the state capitals. This state and local orientation was reinforced by parochialism. Parochial means "local" and "of the parish." Liberals tend to view parochialism as inferior to cosmopolitanism. But to conservatives, parochialism is a virtue.

All this was to change. All the factors that helped produce the collapse of the New Deal coalition also help explain the mobilization of conservatism on a national scale. For the first time, beginning in the 1970s, these locally oriented citizens, normally separated from each other by their parochialism, discovered a shared national experience: the 1960s policy agenda of the Democratic party, particularly the Civil Rights movement.

To jump ahead one decade, this conservative mobilization became the Reagan Revolution. Until Ronald Reagan came along, no one had been able to bring together the various parts of conservative America. This was no easy task because there were so many schisms and fault lines. Mainstream Protestants feared and distrusted the more emotional Evangelical Protestants. Northern Protestants distrusted Southern Protestants. Although they were to come together on the abortion issue, Protestants traditionally distrusted Catholics. Sun Belt conservatives were separated not only by their geographical distance but also by their more secular outlook. Conservative intellectuals, especially the influential neoconservatives, were even more secular and were associated with Ivy League universities and Northeastern cultural elites. And few if any of these conservative components were at home with the mainstream of the Republican party, that is, the liberal mainstream. A number of efforts were made during the 1970s to bring all these conservative components together in a single movement. Moral Majority is the best-known example. But there was no genuine coming together until Ronald Reagan.

Reagan did not create the conservative movement—far from it. But he was the political catalyst who made a national mixture, or coalition, of conservatives possible, and, miracle of miracles, brought it into the Republican party.[6] The new national coalition that was created would be broad enough (encompassing boxes 1, 3, and 4 of Figure 4) and powerful enough to replace the New Deal coalition.

It is widely recognized that the New Deal coalition was built on contradictions—most of its cracks followed from the initial ideological contradictions between the dominant New liberalism and the minority of primarily Southern conservativism. But the Republican coalition was also built upon contradictions. Reagan kept the coalition together throughout the 1980s with a combination of carefully chosen policy proposals and a winning personality. But without Reagan in 1988, the stresses and strains among the coalition partners began to emerge. Pat Robertson's 1988 campaign against George Bush for the Republican presidential nomination was indicative of these strains. Although the Bush campaign leaders had anticipated Robertson's candidacy in time to minimize its effect, they had underestimated the size and strength of the Right, especially the Christian

[6]For a brief but informative account of this process and Reagan's role in it, see Benjamin Ginsberg and Martin Shefter, "A Critical Realignment? The New Politics, the Reconstituted Right, and the 1984 Election," in *The Elections of 1984*, ed. Michael Nelson (Washington: Congressional Quarterly Inc., 1985), pp. 20–24. In the same volume, see also Theodore Lowi, "An Aligning Election, a Presidential Plebiscite," pp. 277–85.

Right. A large number of conservatives never accepted Bush as a genuine conservative. And in fact he wasn't; Bush was a Yankee liberal capitalist who struggled to hold Reagan's construction together. Conservatives stayed formally in the fold, but they felt neglected if not downright betrayed by Bush, and there were frequent intimations of a revolt, or a withdrawal, or another insurgency against Bush for the nomination in 1992. That insurgency came in the form of Pat Buchanan, whose attack on Bush was savage, personal, and ideological. And although Buchanan did no better in the 1992 primary vote than Robertson had done in 1988, Buchanan had a much deeper and more lasting effect. The first indications of this were at the 1992 convention itself. In the days before the opening of the Republican convention in Houston, President Bush virtually lost control of the platform; it became the property of the right wing of the party, and it was more genuinely conservative than any Republican platform in this era, perhaps in this century. The tenuousness of Bush's command of the convention and the party was indicated by the parade of speeches from the Right on the opening night of the convention, during prime time television. Coming so shortly after the airing of the harshly conservative Republican platform, the opening speeches by Pat Buchanan, Pat Robertson, and Marilyn Quayle put an unmistakably right-wing coloration on the entire Republican party. It was no longer the party of the free market and a minimally regulated capitalism that happened to have a right wing attached to it. It was now a party with two equal wings, and with two equal wings it could fly, and would fly with the banner of family values, fortress America, and cultural warfare.

Republicans lost in 1992, and their party leaders will not be able to forget that the loss was in some part attributable to the freshly strengthened influence of the Right. There had to be more to the loss than that, for after all, 62 percent of the votes were cast against Bush, when you combine the Clinton vote and the Perot vote. But it did at first blush appear as though the strong tilt to the right could have put an end not only to George Bush's career but to the Reagan coalition itself after a mere twelve years of ascendancy.

That impression would not last for long. If anything, the 1992 election had cemented the Republican coalition more tightly together than before.

Now that we have some years of perspective on the Reagan/Republican coalition, we can venture to guess that it amounted to a genuine realignment in American politics. A realignment is defined as an election in which a substantial and meaningful segment of the electorate switches from, say, Party A to Party B and then stays loyal to Party B in successive elections. By its nature, the fact of a realignment cannot be known until successive elections have taken place and the realigned vote remains. By definition, Republican victory in five out of six presidential elections from 1968 to 1992 did not amount to a realignment because voters predominantly favored Democrats for congressional and state races. This phenomenon occurred to such an extent that many political scientists were characterizing American politics as having entered a state of "dealignment."[7]

---

[7] The term *dealignment* was coined by Everett Carll Ladd, in "On Mandates, Realignment, and the 1984 Presidential Election," *Political Science Quarterly* 100 (Spring 1985), p. 17. For an instructive discussion of realignment and dealignment, see Howard L. Reiter, *Parties and Elections in Corporate America*, 2d ed. (White Plains, NY: Longman, 1993), Chapter 13.

But it seems that the pundits were all looking in the right direction but through the wrong end of the telescope. We had gotten our realignment, but it was not electoral. We had gotten an *ideological realignment* without an electoral realignment. The Democratic party, in losing most of its Southern conservatives, became almost purely a New liberal party, retreating almost exclusively to box 2 of Figure 4. The Republicans took in the conservative leadership and many of the conservative voters, and as a consequence conservative influence was magnified in the country at large. Conservatives had finally developed a "critical mass"—picture a well-balanced scale where the last tiny unit added to one side tips the scale abruptly, as though the last unit were extremely heavy. Such was the effect of the conservatives joining forces with the traditional Republican party. And thus, the onset of the Republican era in American politics, which to many appeared relatively sudden, was actually the culmination of a development of perhaps more than two decades.

The New Power Structure and the Clinton Presidency

Although Bill Clinton has been criticized by many as being excessively liberal, his political acumen must have sensed that he presided in a Republican era. An analysis of the shift in his agenda from his first year in office to his second year in office indicates as much. This shift explains, in part, Clinton's vacillation on issues and inability to form a coherent vision for his policy programs. Yet if Clinton wants to produce a record of accomplishment, he *must* preside over a Republican agenda. Clinton himself seemed fully aware of this, even early in his presidency.

By April 1993, three months into the new administration, it had become clear to President Clinton that he was going to have to revise his campaign plans, including the middle-class tax cut. He found that he would also have to cast his lot completely with deficit reduction and with NAFTA, or else incur the opposition not only of the Republicans but also of some of his own party members as well as of many influentials on Wall Street, particularly those in the bond market. The following is an intimate account of Clinton at this critical and disillusioning moment:

> "Where are all the Democrats?" Clinton bellowed. "I hope you're all aware we're all Eisenhower Republicans," he said, his voice dripping with sarcasm. "We're Eisenhower Republicans here, and we are fighting the Reagan Republicans. We stand for lower deficits and free trade on the bond market. Isn't that great?"[8]

Table 2 is a pictorial overview of the Clinton transformation. It includes most of the essential policies and policy proposals of the first two years of his administration. The columns and x's are our best judgment as to the main source of support for each of these policy issues.

A superficial glance at Table 2 might give the impression that Clinton's policy agenda did move "to the right" as the months rolled by. It is demonstrably true that fewer x's show up in the New liberal column, and more show up in the Old liberal column and still more in the Conservative column as one moves from year one to year two. But further reflection indicates that the fact that a greater num-

[8]Bob Woodward, *The Agenda: Inside the Clinton White House* (New York: Simon & Schuster, 1994), p. 165.

TABLE 2

The Clinton Agenda: Policy Issues and their Supporting Constituencies

	Policies	Interests Served		
		New Liberal	Old Liberal	Conservative
Year One	Gays in military	x		
	Campaign finance reform	x		
	Deficit reduction as priority		x	x
	Tax on top incomes	x		
	Spending cuts, domestic		x	
	Spending cuts, defense	x		
	Spending increases—"investments"	x		
	Earned income tax credit	x		
	Gas tax (v. Btu tax)		x	
	Brady gun control	x		
	NAFTA		x	
	Motor-Voter	x		
	Family leave	x		
	National service			x
Year Two	Welfare reform		x	x
	Pro–capital punishment			x
	Crime control bill		x	x
	Reinventing government		x	x
	GATT		x	
	Health care reform	x		
	"Accommodation" on school prayer			x

ber of New liberal policies appeared at the beginning was more a result of opportunity and accident than of any ideological time line. For example, although
one of his campaign promises was to change military policy regarding gays, it was
the opposition that forced the issue early in his administration, far earlier than
Clinton had wanted. The items that were included in deficit-reduction proposals
came early because of the requirements of the budget process. The Family Leave
bill, the Brady gun-control bill, and NAFTA had been on Congress's agenda
throughout most of Bush's administration and were ripe for passage as soon as a
Democrat became president. Likewise, proposals like health care reform and welfare reform came later simply because they were recent arrivals on the agenda,
they were far too complicated to yield to simple proposals, and it was going to
take time for Clinton's "task forces" to bring together supportive data and a supportive constituency for such controversial matters.

Thus, although there is a chronological element in Table 2, that chronology in
itself is not a portrait of Bill Clinton. The real Bill Clinton is the whole table—all
of the policy items taken together. And when we look at this whole picture, it is
difficult to determine from his policies whether Clinton is a Democrat or
whether he is a Republican. Senator-elect Fred Thompson (R-TN) was more
correct than even he was probably aware in his response to President Clinton's

December 1994 speech from the Oval Office announcing his "Middle Class Bill of Rights," promising the middle-class tax cut that he had backed away from his first year in office. Thompson said that he was happy Clinton had endorsed the Republican position and that if Clinton was serious he could lead the Republicans, but if he was not serious he would have to follow the Republicans.

If the intellectual hegemony of the new Republican coalition had not fully proven itself before the November election, most of the remaining doubts were dispelled by it. In fact, some could now be led to the conclusion that the long-awaited *electoral realignment* had now come to pass. Capture of the entire Congress after forty-two years is not even the most impressive support for the hypothesis of electoral realignment. After all, dramatic as it appears to be for the Republicans to be able to organize the House of Representatives, this only required a switch of 12 percent of the seats in the House from Democratic to Republican, with the national decline of the Democratic vote from 52.9 percent in 1990 to 50.8 percent in 1992 to 46.4 percent in 1994. Meanwhile, most surveys report that the numbers of self-identified Republicans and Democrats are about equal. No, the telling evidence for possible electoral realignment can be found in the votes for governors and state legislatures, as reported earlier.

Only a succession of several elections will tell the whole story. Prediction of an electoral realignment is perilous, and in fact it is the most knowledgeable observers who ought to be the ones most in suspense about this particular epoch. Maintenance of the Republican-dominated national power structure depends upon the maintenance of those 1994 electoral majorities, and that in turn depends upon the ability of Republican leaders to keep their coalition from breaking up, comprising as it does such deeply contradictory ideologies and interests. This particular national coalition and the uncertainty of its longevity will go far in defining the future of the political process itself, as far into the new century as we can reasonably project.

We are now ready to assess the real Bill Clinton that this policy portrait has shown us and the significance of his administration for our system at the end of the century.

BILL CLINTON: A MAN FOR THE CENTER

No American politician has ever had a more publicly discussed character than Bill Clinton. In fact, it is doubtful whether anyone's private life has ever been more publicly displayed than that of Bill Clinton. But is is not Bill Clinton's social or moral character that concerns us here; it is his political character.

The overall pattern of policy choices in the Clinton agenda indicates that Clinton was a man born for the Center. This fact was captured by the distinguished journalist William Greider, who observed that

> A president who is serious about fostering fundamental change must be prepared to stand alone against the status quo and bravely insist on first principles. . . . Ronald

Reagan was such a president. He was continually derided as pigheaded and oblivious to reality (he was both), [yet his] stubbornness profoundly altered the political landscape.

[Clinton] chose a different course: He made common cause with selected power blocs—congressional barons of the Democratic Party and major corporate-financial interests normally aligned with the Republicans as well as those right-of-center Southern Democrats who are traditionally pro-visionists and anti-labor. The strategy assumed that once Clinton had satisfied their particular needs, these forces would help him to prevail on crucial reform issues. Instead, they ate his lunch.[9]

Greider went on to observe that even Clinton's commitment to campaign and political-party reform was marginal, because "instead of flogging Congress and the entrenched interests on the scandal of political money, Clinton ceded the issue to congressional Democrats, who, not surprisingly, do not wish to alter the status quo since it works for them." Although Clinton did make his cabinet and top appointments "look more like America," he nevertheless filled the fiscal areas of his government with Wall Street Democrats, who, "not surprisingly, defined *new Democrat* in their own terms." Consequently, Clinton's basic economic policy, "despite the partisan bombast from Republicans," is actually not all that different from George Bush's. "Clinton embraced the argument that deficit reduction must be his first priority" so that, with this established, other, more substantial matters could be accomplished. Clinton's most important victory in the first two years, the passage of NAFTA, was accomplished with Republican votes over the opposition of most Democrats. "The logic that led Clinton into this cul-de-sac sounded plausible, but it was a trap. A Democratic president with activist inclinations, he was told, had to demonstrate that he was preparing to be 'responsible' about curbing the deficits."[10]

Greider's characterization is to a great extent confirmed by the pattern of policy choices in the Clinton agenda. As we said before, Clinton is a man born for the Center. He has sought the Center as a place to maximize affections, he has sought the Center as the place where compromises are made, and he has sought the Center because that is where leadership is and can be exerted. In fact, Clinton behaves as though where he is *is* the Center. He has spent his whole political life building the big tent—or, as Jonathan Swift put it 250 years ago, the "suit of cloaths that invests everything."

But just as the "spectrum," or the single continuum with all beliefs ranged tidily step by step from left to right, is a fiction, so is any traditional idea of the Center itself. What is "the Center"? The Center is certainly not the midpoint between two ideological positions, because most of the time there are more than two ideological positions and rarely a prior agreement on precisely what to disagree about. In fact, the definition of what to disagree about is the most creative part of the policy-making process, and this is not accomplished by staking out a center but by careful examination of the foundations and arguments of each and every position. No, for a person like Clinton who believes there is a center, the Center is simply a gathering place for people who are without ideology, who

[9]William Greider, "Clinton at Midterm: What Went Wrong?" *Rolling Stone*, 3 November 1994, p. 48.
[10]The various quotes are from Ibid., p. 108.

come to the party with their narrowly defined interests and check their ideologies and ideas at the door before entering. The Center comprises all the people with access to the political process, who speak for their own interests or the interests of their clients or constituents and are easily willing to compromise to achieve these interests. Nearly thirty years ago, one of the authors of this book coined a phrase to characterize what the liberalism of the New Deal had become after too many years in power: *interest-group liberalism*. We can still call it liberal because it remained optimistic and dedicated to using government conscientiously to help those least able to help themselves. But it had grown decadent in allowing anyone with a special interest a place at the table. This was politics based on the principle of "to each according to his claim."[11] That is Bill Clinton's Center today—not a center of balanced forces and of compromise among previously articulated positions, but the politics of accommodation of claims whose foundations don't matter very much.

The problem with interest-group liberalism is that, although its practitioners have been successful in achieving their legislative aims, as a principle of government, interest-group liberalism has proven to be self-defeating. It allows for no capacity to say "No." It transforms *every* claim into a right. It precludes the development of priorities, even among members of the same party. The absence of priorities is why it is so difficult to make sense of any major public policy proposals or enactments of recent years.

Take a single example: the 1994 crime bill, which we discussed in Chapter 2 as an example of symbolic politics. In its final form, the bill represented an agglomeration of hundreds of different interests. It contained 409 Sections with 32 Titles. There is so much material in the statute that it includes not only a seven-page, two-column table of contents, but also a three-page, two-column index. While many bills that are passed by Congress are omnibus bills covering various matters, this bill is all on crime. It nevertheless masqueraded as one unified, lawful approach to America's most pressing problem. In reality, it is an array of claims that survived the legislative obstacle course. It is a bill without vision, without a point of view, without coherence.

For example, one of the liberal aims of the act is Title XI, Subtitle A, Sec. 110102, Paragraph (v) (1), which states, "It shall be unlawful for a person to manufacture, transfer, or possess a semiautomatic assault weapon." Nothing could be simpler or more direct. This is a genuine rule of law, and it is directed toward a problem widely recognized in studies of crime. But it is followed immediately by Paragraph (v) (2): "Paragraph (1) shall not apply to possession or transfer of any semiautomatic assault weapon otherwise lawfully possessed under Federal law on the date of the enactment of this subsection [and] (3) Paragraph (1) shall not apply to—(A) *any of the firearms or replicas or duplicates of the firearms, specified in Appendix A to this section. . . ."* A look at Appendix A reveals a categorized listing of over seven hundred automatic assault weapons *to be exempted from the prohibition.* And with these seven hundred exemptions there is the following proviso: "*The fact that a firearm is not listed in Appendix A shall not be construed to mean that Paragraph (1) applies to such firearm."* (Emphasis added.)

---

[11]Theodore Lowi, "The Public Philosophy: Interest-Group Liberalism," *American Political Science Review*, March 1967; and Lowi, *The End of Liberalism*, (New York: W. W. Norton, 1969).

A second example is drawn from two other titles of the act; these will help explain how such a large agglomeration with so many exemptions as the one above could have been adopted in the first place. Title I, Part Q, is entitled "Cops on the Beat." It provides federal grants "to increase police presence . . . and otherwise to enhance public safety," and gives discretion as to the distribution of these grants to the Attorney General. There is virtually no vision, and there are no guidelines or even suggestions of guidelines for the Attorney General to observe in the distribution of these funds. Approximately $9 billion was authorized to be appropriated over six years, beginning in 1995. The second part of this example comes under Title III, Subtitle A, entitled "Ounce of Prevention Council." This council is to be composed of several cabinet-level officials and is authorized by the statute to spend just under $90 million over the six years beginning in 1995 on any local program which, in the council's opinion, might help prevent crime.

It is amazing how often Congress attempts to compensate for the absence of genuine law and of policy vision in a statute by inventing cute and wishful titles for those statutes. We often do the same in foreign policy adventures, such as Desert Storm and Operation Save Democracy, but at least a foreign policy action requires an immediate public appeal to Americans. In a domestic program that is going to involve a tremendous amount of effort over six or more years to alter people's conduct and to alter the priorities of local government budgets, these statutes must have some simple, operative principles and not just simply list a series of items that have nothing in common.

There is much more to the Crime Act of 1994, but the point here has already been made, perhaps excessively: The Crime Act of 1994 is really a picture of what *the Center* looks like. To quote Gertrude Stein, "There is no there there." And that's precisely what Bill Clinton has been searching for.

The more important health care reform bill could easily have served as another example of what the Center looks like. President Clinton used over a year and a task force of five hundred technocrats headed by Hillary Clinton to write an extremely large and unwieldy legislative proposal totalling 1,342 pages. But instead of holding to the four or five clear principles of reform in this proposal, Clinton immediately began to compromise with both Democrats and Republicans, especially in the Senate. As a result, there were four major alternatives that came out of congressional committees and some parts of all of them ultimately were incorporated in the bill that came to the floor. Although some important principles were left in the bill, there was nothing cumulative or focused in it, and nothing that gave the president a clear platform on which to stand or on which Democratic candidates for re-election to Congress could run.

It should be emphasized that this is not a partisan point, nor is it a point limited to President Clinton. For example, the 1990 reform and revision of the original Clean Air Act, passed during George Bush's presidency, was 718 pages long! Although it is filled with very specific instructions to the Environmental Protection Agency (EPA) on how and what to regulate, these are loosely joined, virtually separate pieces of action that still required the EPA to issue at least 50 major and 30 minor regulations within the two succeeding years in order to implement the rather ambiguous intent of Congress.[12] Examples such as these have led one political scientist to observe that "American public bureaucracy is not designed to be effective" but rather to advance the interests of "those who've exercised political power."[13]

77

THE NEW
POLITICAL
PROCESS: FROM
INNOVATIONAL
TO INCREMENTAL
POLITICS

Thus, the Center is composed of any type of act, important or unimportant, that is written to accommodate a maximum number of involved interests. An old example that is coming up for renewal in 1995 is the Magnuson Fisheries Act of 1976, whose purpose was to protect American fishing by creating and regulating a two-hundred-mile "exclusive economic zone" around the U.S. coastline. But rather than make the law itself, Congress set up eight regional councils to manage each of eight newly created fishing regions by setting their own catch limits, etc. But it put the councils officially in the hands of those people most involved in the fishing business itself.[14] As one observer put it, "It is as if Weyerhaeuser, the nation's largest private logging company, were able to dictate how many trees could be cut in the national forests, and then took the timber without paying a dime for it."[15] This is government by conflict-of-interest. This is the Center.

THE NEW POLITICAL PROCESS: FROM INNOVATIONAL TO INCREMENTAL POLITICS

Interest-group liberalism contributed to the collapse of the New Deal coalition toward the end of the 1960s, because *everything* became good to do. The unguided growth and the attempts to accommodate every interest magnified the contradictions within the coalition, and deepened fissures in the cement that had held it together for thirty years. The causes of the collapse of the New Deal coalition can shed some light on the future of the coalition that replaced it—the Reagan/Republican coalition. For it, too, is built on contradictions that will eventually cause its collapse.

Before we can predict when and how the Republican coalition will collapse, we need to ask, what holds it together? Belonging to the same party helps. The party provides opportunity, money, recognition, legitimacy, and a ready-made audience—all invaluable resources to intellectuals of whatever persuasion. But simple party identification is not enough, especially not in a coalition of the Republican type. Because it is composed of ideas, and since many of these ideas are contradictory, the Republican coalition must ultimately persist or perish by ideas.

Look first at why the realism of party support is inadequate. We can evaluate its inadequacy by comparing the Republican coalition to the New Deal coali-

---

[12]David Shoenbrod, *Power Without Responsibility: How Congress Abuses the People through Delegation* (New Haven: Yale University Press, 1993), pp. 80–81.

[13]Ibid., p. 81.

[14]*Magnuson Fishery Conservation and Management Act*, Public Law 94-265 (13 April 1976), 90 Stat. 331.

[15]Timothy Egan, "Hook, Line and Sunk," *New York Times Magazine*, 11 December 1994, p. 78.

tion. First of all, although there were important and influential intellectuals in the New Deal coalition, and although they did share a common vision, this made the Democratic party the party of *innovation*, and innovation meant expansion of the national government as a sign of its responsiveness to the needs and demands of the American people. But politically, that gave each component of the coalition hope of reward. They must hang together, or they would ultimately hang separately. What this means in the most stark, realistic terms is that the New Deal coalition held itself together to a large extent through patronage or the expectation of patronage. Now mind you, patronage does not simply mean giving out jobs to job seekers. That's the least important form of patronage. The patronage available to the Democratic party was the patronage of favorable government policies and favorable government decisions regarding the application of those policies—the awarding of construction contracts, or the handing out of inside information, for example. Thus, the Democratic party of the New Deal was still a nineteenth-century patronage party, albeit modernized by the addition of some important programmatic commitments that the nineteenth-century parties managed to avoid.

Second, with the liberals leading the New Deal coalition, the policy approach was going to be instrumental. This meant that policies were evaluated by analyzing the costs and benefits of each policy's consequences. This also meant that compromise among conflicting interests was facilitated and found. This is the same Center that Bill Clinton has been looking for, but there was more consensus about this in the vigorous early days of the New Deal coalition.

Third, the Cold War and national security concerns shored up the new institution of the strong presidency. In addition to giving the presidency a strong and highly supportive public opinion base, it also gave the Democratic party a good twenty-year headstart in tying corporate interests, especially defense-oriented corporations, to the Democratic party.

Now compare the cement of the New Deal coalition to that of the Republican coalition. Today, patronage is far, far less available, government has not been innovational for over twenty years, and there is no prospect of government growth that could give the party in power a special advantage. But more important in this regard is the fact that Republicans are, in principle, against the growth of government and against the use of government for political purposes. The one area of government growth Republicans could accept is the area of national defense, but growth through new programs in this area was already winding down dramatically even before defense expenditures themselves began to decline. Since the collapse of the Soviet Union in 1989, it will be virtually impossible to establish new programs even if Republicans succeed in reviving defense expenditures. (Intimations of that revival have already come in late 1994, with President Clinton's announcement that he was adding $25 billion to the defense budget.)

The Negation of National Government

So, with patronage, innovation, and growth ruled out, what's left? What holds the parts of the Republican coalition together? The key cementing factor seems to be *the principle of negation of government itself.*

An idea of this sort is not as superficial as it first may appear to be. And the point of view has certainly become ubiquitous. For example, President Clinton's entire "Middle Class Bill of Rights" was based upon negation. In the first place, the proposal was essentially a series of tax cuts that would permit middle-income people to retain a few hundred dollars more of their yearly income, if used for certain desirable purposes. But even more to the point, Clinton went on to say,

79

THE NEW
POLITICAL
PROCESS: FROM
INNOVATIONAL
TO INCREMENTAL
POLITICS

> We can pay for this middle-class Bill of Rights by continuing to reduce Government spending. . . . We can sell off entire operations the Government no longer needs to run and turn dozens of programs over to states and communities that know best how to solve their own problems.
>
> My plan will save billions of dollars from the Energy Department, cut down the Transportation Department and shrink 60 programs into 4 at the Department of Housing and Urban Development.
>
> Our reinventing government initiative . . . already has helped to shrink bureaucracy and free up money to pay down the deficit and invest in our people. Already we've passed budgets to reduce the Federal Government to its smallest size in 30 years and to cut the deficit by $700 billion.[16]

Except for making a tax cut appear to be a right, the entire text of Clinton's speech, which set the tone for the second two years of his term, could have come from any major Republican in the past forty years. The Republicans' policy of no policy has been elevated to the level of political philosophy. It is genuinely the condition for cohesion between Old liberals and conservatives. To the Old liberals, anarchists at heart, *all* government is bad and should be negated to the extent possible. To conservatives, some government is good, as long as it is run by good people who make good decisions and who are guided by morality. The conservatives are true "statists," but they envision good government as best serving Americans at the *state* level; these conservatives are genuinely anti-*national* government. Although comfortable with a welfare state, and comfortable with many national government efforts to put some restraints on capitalism and competition, conservatives have become increasingly resentful and alarmed over the efforts by the New liberals to set "national standards" for many categories of conduct that conservatives place in the realm of private and community power, over which only the state governments have constitutional power (in the opinion of the conservatives).

Consequently, the Old liberals and the genuine conservatives can make common cause against the national government. Negation of the national government is the common policy, the common vision, and therefore the cohesive element of the Republican coalition.

Their common cause has been reinforced by the habit reaching back a number of years of referring to Old liberals as conservative. It should be clear by now to readers of this chapter that such a reference is profoundly incorrect. But it does help mask the underlying contradictions between Old liberalism and conservatism, and it masks the reality even from those who ought to know better.

Finally, negation as a public philosophy has been validated and reinforced by the times in which we live. With the collapse of the New Deal coalition, the

[16]From text of president's 15 December 1994 address to the nation, printed in the *New York Times*, 16 December 1994, p. A36.

epoch of substantial innovation was over. No more major new programs were established after the Great Society binge of the late 60s and early 70s. Nor were any major programs eliminated. The only two identifiable programs that disappeared were the Civil Aeronautics Board under President Carter and the Comprehensive Employment Training Administration under President Reagan. Considering the past twelve years of sound and fury against big government and the alarm expressed at increases in the annual deficit, the fact that there were no big innovations up or down is truly amazing. The one exception might be the Reagan tax reforms in 1981 and 1986, but although these cuts were substantial they were the essence of negation of government. After a number of years of non-innovation, the Republican antigovernment message began to sound increasingly plausible. Moreover, the Republican promise of better management and of opposition to bureaucracy began to sound appealing, even to those who had a big stake in one or more programs.

The Politics of Incrementalism

Another prominent feature of the times in which we live has been the routinization of what came to be called "divided government." There was divided government for six years of the Eisenhower administration, and there was divided government during all eight years of presidents Nixon and Ford. By the time of the second Reagan administration and the Bush administration, divided government had become a working feature of the American political process. But divided government was important mainly because of the impact it had on the perspectives and strategies of the two major political parties. Since it was rare for either party to capture the entire national government—especially with sufficient margin to govern—and since each had safe haven in one or more chambers or branches of the national government, each party came to view itself as the majority party. National government had become a duopoly, as when two companies dominate a single market. The theory of duopoly holds that neither company will have much incentive to take the substantial risks that are involved in substantial innovation.

Likewise, in the political world, the two major parties not only have grown accustomed to the politics of incrementalism, they also have the same incentives as duopolistic companies to perpetuate the politics of incrementalism. This is not a commitment as such to the status quo, even though it may have that effect. The draconian rhetoric of the new Republican majority in Congress is in fact sincerely antagonistic to the status quo. But the Republicans share with President Clinton and the Democrats an unwillingness to alter the established structure of government or of policy. Leaving aside this steadfast refusal of Republican leaders to specify how they intend to balance the budget by 2002, the truth is in their actions: They are going after the margins—a 1 percent cut here, a 5 percent cut there, a billion-dollar cut here, a $280-million cut there—all amounting to fractions of a percent downward but all equally and consistently expressing a negative posture toward the national government. There is no genuine restructuring. And there is no effort whatsoever to restructure the party system that produces this institutionalized commitment to incrementalism.

Although incrementalism is favored by both parties at this time, a whole epoch of incrementalist politics is far more to the advantage of Republicans than Democrats, because voters expect innovation from Democrats and not from Republicans. The gridlock that was so criticized during the 1992 campaign was not gridlock at all, but was the Republican policy of no policies. It was a position held by many if not most mainstream Republicans even under President Nixon, but it could not become a leading viewpoint as long as New liberalism remained hegemonic. Change toward this view was discernible even under President Carter, though at first it was interpreted as post-Watergate trauma, or legitimacy crisis, in response to which President Carter was promising to make American government as good as the American people. It became the prevailing viewpoint with President Reagan, drawing in the "Boll Weevil" Democrats and then more of the mainstream Democrats, along with the Republicans in Congress.

As the Republican coalition came into its own, the politics slid more and more toward incrementalism and the institutional advantage slipped more and more toward Congress. We are still a presidential government, make no mistake about that. But the presidency, like the Democratic party, thrives on the politics of innovation. Innovation is expected of the president, and most of the risks and payoffs of innovation have accrued to the presidency, regardless of the party of the person occupying the office. The incrementalism of this epoch is so strong that presidents, seeking innovation, have had to avoid Congress altogether.

One of the best demonstrations of the president's need for innovation, and of the president's tendency to avoid Congress in order to get it, is Ronald Reagan's approach to one of his most important campaign promises—deregulation. Although Reagan was genuinely committed to deregulation, he did not confront Congress with a single legislative proposal to terminate any regulatory agency. If he had tried to do so, he would have had to confront a House of Representatives controlled by the Democrats, and he would also have had to confront a wide array of interest groups who would have fought him in order to defend a particular program. Instead, Reagan issued Executive Order 12291, which required that all proposals for new regulations generated by the executive branch be reviewed by the Office of Management and Budget. This executive order and the process it set up required "presidential oversight of the regulatory process," and that gave President Reagan leverage to reduce or reject rules and regulations without having to terminate any agencies. During his two terms in office, Reagan managed to cut almost in half the number of rules and regulations appearing for implementation in the *Federal Register*.[17] In essence, President Reagan got what he wanted by avoiding Congress and the interest-group process altogether.

It would be a mistake to view Reagan's deregulation by management strategy as a case of a Republican president avoiding a Democratic Congress in the era of divided government. That is part of the explanation, but the phenomenon is bigger than that. Presidents of either party now have increasing incentive, or even need, to flank Congress, regardless of which party holds the majority of seats. For not

81

THE NEW
POLITICAL
PROCESS: FROM
INNOVATIONAL
TO INCREMENTAL
POLITICS

[17]The *Federal Register* (begun in 1935) is the daily publication of all official acts of Congress, the president, and the administrative agencies. A law or executive order is not legally binding until published in the *Federal Register*.

only does a president tend to lose when going up against Congress, working with Congress will actually draw the president into the politics of incrementalism.

Incrementalism is not only built into the duopolistic relationship between the two majority-bent parties; it is institutionalized in Congress's own rules. When the Gramm-Rudman deficit-reduction act was passed, most of the public attention focused on the "sequestration provisions" that required the imposition of automatic spending cuts if the projected deficit for fiscal year 1987 was not reduced to $154 billion or below. Less notice was given to what appears now to be a more important aspect of that act: the revision of congressional rules, especially those in the Senate, providing that a supplemental spending bill is out of order if it is not "deficit neutral"—in other words, it must demonstrate that it proposes cuts equal to the proposed spending. This converted congressional policymaking into what came to be called a "zero-sum game," where every spending action had to be accompanied by an equal and opposite cutting reaction.

When this newly institutionalized incremental system came to roost on President Clinton, he was enraged, according to Bob Woodward, that these petty rules were going to decimate his multi-billion-dollar investment program. Clinton's investments, according to Woodward, "had been decimated because of the caps on spending for years 1994 and 1995 that had been part of the 1990 budget deal. In 1990, the caps seemed a wonderful way to get some $100 billion in future deficit reduction without any immediate pain. But the future had arrived and the caps were now an iron clad reality."[18] This was the Gramm-Rudman spirit visiting the very type of president Senators Gramm and Rudman had envisioned. Clinton was absolutely enraged. "It was instantly apparent that the president didn't grasp what had happened. The magnitude and import of the House's action had never sunk in. . . . Slamming his fist down on the end of his chair, Clinton let loose a torrent of rage and frustration. He said he felt blindsided. This was totally inconsistent with what he had been told. Why hadn't they ever had a serious discussion about the caps? . . . Clinton and his administration had once again settled into a state of lessened expectations."[19]

Symbolic politics, such as the Crime Control Act of 1994, are often also incrementalist politics. Control of government and the deficit by budgetary ceilings, expenditure caps, rescissions, etc., is a way of appearing to fight the deficit without eliminating entire programs, i.e., without making substantive policy decisions. A 1 percent, or even a 5 percent cut across the board is playing with the margins of very large systems, where even numbers that appear very large are, in relative terms, quite small. Likewise with reinventing government: Cutting two hundred thousand employees over four years out of nearly three million in the Civil Service is incremental—and it is also extra-congressional.

Another case that can have important consequences but that is nevertheless a case of incrementalism is the Federal Reserve Board's setting of monetary policy through control of interest and discount rates. Here a vastly powerful and autonomous national agency relies on tiny fractional percentage changes up or down to head off inflation or otherwise to fine-tune the economy. And no Congress *or* president can intervene.

[18]The account of the "zero-sum game" introduced by Gramm-Rudman is from Jonathan Rauch, "Zero-Sum Budget Game," *National Journal*, 10 May 1986, p. 1096. The Bob Woodward quote is from *The Agenda*, pp. 155–56.

[19]Woodward, *The Agenda*, pp. 161–62, 170.

Finally, take the most recent case, the Contract with America (see Box 2, page 34) proclaimed by the House Republicans before the 1994 election and claimed as a mandate after the electoral victory. On the surface, the Contract with America may appear innovative. But closer analysis reveals it to be based on the politics of incrementalism. Before going into the details of the contract, note that the promise was not to *enact* but to *introduce* bills and get some action within the first one hundred days of the new Congress. Note also that the contract adheres loyally to the Republican public philosophy of the negation of national government. Now to a closer look.

The first three items (the Fiscal Responsibility Act, the Taking Back Our Streets Act, and the Personal Responsibility Act) propose generalized spending cuts, without specifying amounts or percentages. But since they are across-the-board expenditure cuts, they are inevitably marginal. The new Republican chair of the House Budget Committee, John Kasich, was bold enough to estimate that Republicans will vote for and then "bank" around $250 billion in spending cuts, spread over five years. Now lay four more items of the Contract against that. The Family Reinforcement Act, the American Dream Restoration Act, the Senior Citizens' Equity Act, and the Job Creation and Wage Enhancement Act are all proposals for tax cuts, and the estimated losses of revenue over five years for these cuts, assuming they are all passed, would total $220 billion. These spending cuts and tax cuts sound like large amounts, but the *net reduction* of the deficit that they would produce is only $30 billion, and when that is spread over the five projected years, it does not amount to a hill of beans, especially in the context of an overall annual national budget approaching $2 trillion. Even if the estimated spending cuts were doubled (as proposed in Clinton's 1993 budget), the net deficit reduction would still be small; when spread across the hundreds of major government programs, no single program is going to be in for much trouble.

One aspect of the Personal Responsibility Act could prove to be exceptional, and it is of particular interest to the conservatives. If adopted as proposed, this reform would stigmatize Aid to Families with Dependent Children (AFDC) and welfare in general by punishing illegitimacy and by limiting assistance to two years. But it does amount to a more substantive innovation. Meanwhile, the Fiscal Responsibility Act proposes to remove major questions of spending and taxation from Congress altogether. And the Taking Back Our Streets Act proposes the clearly incremental change of modifying the anti-crime sanctions already provided in the 1994 Crime Control Act. There are few net expenditure cuts proposed here; the act is really just a move from Clinton's approach of crime-prevention through investment toward crime prevention through deterrence—more prisons and punishment. The last two proposals are strictly marginal, and largely symbolic. They would mandate (an ugly word to most Republicans) to the states some important changes in the treatment of product liability laws and establish term limits "to replace career politicians with citizen legislators."

Bob Woodward observed toward the end of Clinton's first two years that his administration had "settled into a state of lessened expectations."[20] But it seems clear from our analysis that his observation could be applied to all presidents of

[20]Ibid., p. 170.

the recent past as well as the near future. Another related generalization is that President Clinton is going to learn fast some of Ronald Reagan's tricks of the trade about bypassing Congress. The so-called bailout of Mexico in late January 1995 gives us a first intimation. Clinton had gone to Congress earlier in the month to get it to approve $40 billion in loan guarantees to stabilize and then reverse the free fall of the Mexican economy. But after a few days, Clinton discarded that request and announced that he would use his own emergency authority to lend up to $20 billion to Mexico to keep it from defaulting on its debts. The president took a far larger personal risk by moving directly rather than bringing Congress along with him, but if it makes the Mexican economy respond positively, as it seems to be doing, then the president will also reap a political benefit. Either way, this case illustrates once again that the separation of powers provided for in the Constitution has become a segregation of power.

WHAT FUTURE FOR AMERICAN POLITICS?

Despite the big 1994 victory, the end of the Republican era is just over the horizon, brought closer by the Republican party's very attainment of power in both chambers of the U.S. Congress. The Republican coalition will ultimately collapse from within, just as the New Deal coalition did, and probably sooner, because it has too little cement. It will collapse when real innovation is needed once again. That need will undoubtedly arise, just as it did in the late 1960s. Or else the coalition will collapse when the traditional Right abandons the Republican party, as it most certainly will as its numbers grow and it is able to reject the godlessness, pragmatism, and acquisitiveness of the Old liberalism of the Republican mainstream. Indeed, the Right's numbers are growing quickly already; it has been estimated that the Republican infantry in at least six hundred state legislative districts was made up of members or affiliates of the Christian Coalition.

Meanwhile, a more dangerous trend could leave democracy—or the republic itself—permanently impaired. In order to sustain a shared belief in the negation of government, the Republican coalition also will have to commit itself to the *negation of politics*. After all, politics is essentially a way to get government to respond, to do things, to take substantive, innovative action. We have already seen the popularity of the negation of politics, not only among gleeful Republicans, but also among determined Perotists and increasingly among loyal Democrats. The most serious examples are proposals for constitutional provisions severely limiting democracy or, should we say, majoritarian politics: constitutional limits on debt and deficits through the balanced budget amendment; the virtual abolition of majority rule on tax policy by requiring a three-fifths vote to increase taxes; constitutionally mandated term limits for members of the House and Senate; and delegation of Congress's remaining real spending powers to the president, through the line-item veto. There are other restrictions on democracy not elevated to constitutional stature but severe nevertheless: the prohibition of unfunded mandates to the states, which will effectively terminate the power of the national government to "set national standards"; and the abolition of majority control of expenditure authority by requiring a three-fifths vote on expenditure items or supplements that are not, in themselves, "budget neutral." Another serious departure from democracy, that is neither constitutional nor statutory but important nonetheless, is the practice whereby both major political parties rely on scandal and other non-electoral methods (which we have called RIP) to neutralize or destroy opposition leaders.

This trend is not something Republicans should take lightly, but they *are* taking it lightly, just as decadent Democrats in the 1960s took much too lightly their obligation to observe constitutional limits on their enthusiasm to do good.

All of the patterns and problems that could be seen vividly in these two short years of the Clinton administration do give us some vision into the future. The age of politics that this country has known for most of its history has ended, and the age of governance has begun. This was inevitable as soon as America developed a big, positive government, much like the governments of Europe. Politics still exists, but it is a very different kind of politics: a boring one of budgets and marginal analysis, technical papers and details. Gone are the joyous politics of movements, demands, claims, responsiveness, and innovation.

This profound change in the nature of politics, which reflects a permanent change in the nature of government, means that the role of each and every institution of democracy has to be redefined. Citizenship must be redefined, away from obedience, consent, and passivity, and toward intelligent criticism. Political parties must be redefined; there is serious doubt that the two-party system can any longer survive its nineteenth-century origins and foundations. The electoral process must be redefined. Is it possible that a multicultural, multiethnic, multiracial country can tolerate a single-member-district system that gives all the winnings to a plurality, and zero winnings to even substantial minorities? The role of Congress must be redefined. No Congress in an enormous and active government can spend inordinate amounts of time on tens of thousands of pieces of trivia, without any genuine and sustained sense of priority. The commitment of the new Republican leadership to the elimination of substantial amounts of congressional staff is a good first step; Congress could never justify a staff of nearly forty thousand professional people. But cutting staff will not be an advancement if it simply means that Congress will cut down on serious activity. It will serve a good purpose only if it frees members of Congress to concern themselves with perhaps no more than half a dozen major legislative issues per session.

And finally, the presidency itself has to be redefined. Certain basic aspects of presidential democracy must be maintained and strengthened. The "bully pulpit" is as much needed in this epoch as at any time in our history. But presidents can no longer indulge themselves in the raw and most vulgar aspects of mass politics. With the disappearance of the cold war, the rallying effect of national security activity, which has been a vital source of popularity and therefore strength for the presidency over the past fifty years, is no longer a dependable resource. Presidents are going to have to become more parliamentary. A government of segregated powers, a relic of the age of politics, cannot survive in the new age of governance.

FOR FURTHER READING

Birnbaum, Jeffrey. *The Lobbyists*. New York: Times Books, 1992.

Calleo, David P. *The Bankrupting of America*. New York: William Morrow, 1992.

Dionne, E. J., Jr. *Why Americans Hate Politics*. New York: Simon and Schuster, 1991.

Draper, Theodore. *A Very Thin Line: The Iran-Contra Affairs*. New York: Hill and Wang, 1991.

Drew, Elizabeth. *On the Edge: The Clinton Presidency*. New York: Simon and Schuster, 1994.

Friedman, Benjamin M. *Day of Reckoning: The Consequences of American Economic Policy under Reagan and After*. New York: Random House, 1988.

Ginsberg, Benjamin, and Martin Shefter. *Politics by Other Means: The Declining Importance of Elections in America*. New York: Basic Books, 1990.

Greider, William. *Who Will Tell the People? The Betrayal of American Democracy*. New York: Simon and Schuster, 1992.

Hertzke, Allen D. *Echoes of Discontent: Jesse Jackson, Pat Robertson, and the Resurgence of Populism*. Washington, DC: Congressional Quarterly Press, 1993.

Jackson, Brooks. *Honest Graft: Big Money and the American Political Process*. Rev. ed. Washington, DC: Farragut Publishing, 1990.

Johnson, Haynes. *Sleepwalking through History: America in the Reagan Years*. New York: W. W. Norton, 1991.

Kernell, Samuel, ed. *Parallel Politics: Economic Policymaking in the United States and Japan*. Washington, DC: Brookings Institution, 1991.

Kurtz, Howard. *Media Circus*. New York: Times Books, 1993.

Kutler, Stanley. *The Wars of Watergate*. New York: W. W. Norton, 1992.

Lowi, Theodore. *The End of Liberalism*. 2d ed. New York: W. W. Norton, 1979.

Phillips, Kevin. *Boiling Point: Democrats, Republicans, and the Decline of Middle-Class Prosperity*. New York: Random House, 1993.

Rosenstone, Steven, and John Mark Hansen. *Mobilization, Participation, and Democracy in America*. New York: Macmillan, 1993.

Sundquist, James L. *Constitutional Reform and Effective Government*. Rev. ed. Washington, DC: Brookings Institution, 1992.

Weaver, R. Kent, and Bert Rockman, eds. *Do Institutions Matter?* Washington, DC: Brookings Institution, 1993.

Woodward, Bob. *The Agenda: Inside the Clinton White House*. New York: Simon and Schuster, 1994.